ISBN 1 899624 28 7
First published in the United Kingdom by Challenger Publications

CW01651572

The Railways in and around

BURTON

UPON TRENT

by

H.N.Twells OBE

Cover picture - **A Leicester-Burton line service arriving at Burton in June 1964 behind Stanier Class 5 No.45444.** Author

Challenger Publications
15 Lovers Lane
Grasscroft
Oldham
OL4 4DP

Printed by Printflow Colour Limited, Bolton.

ACKNOWLEDGEMENTS

As a Burtonian, my interest in the town's railways goes back an awful long time, and I have been fortunate in being able to collect a comprehensive collection of photographs and other material relating to the railways serving the town.

We all owe an immense debt of gratitude to those who became photographers, and turned their lens to record the railway scene, albeit that the vast bulk of such material is post 1945. However, it is important that scenes and information of a bygone age are recorded for future generations, and we must each make our small contribution to the historical record. Had they not spent their time and hard-earned money, recording the then 'present', we would not now be able to enjoy the delights of the past railway era.

I would like to express my sincere thanks to the photographers who have loaned photographs for inclusion in this book: Tommy Tomalin; Patrick Webb; Paul A.Forbes; Roger Newman; Peter Stevenson; Robin Jeffcoat; Mr A.O.Wynn; Allan Sommerfield; Roy Anderson; Michael King; Eric Woods; the late E.R.Morten; Mr R.C.Riley; Bernard Holland; David Gilbert; Gordon Coltas; John Miller; John Edgington; Ken Fairey; Geoff Barnett; Bill Stubbs; Roy Burrows Collection; Philip Millard; Ben Brooksbank; A.Henshaw; Tim Shuttleworth; J.S.Simnett; the late H.N.James; M.Woodcock; and the late Mr H.C.Casserley. I am most grateful to them all, and trust that if I have inadvertently omitted anyone, they will accept my sincere apologies. Thanks also to Brian Radford for supplying, at short notice, material relating to the former Midland Railway.

My very sincere thanks too to Challenger Publications for their interest and support in publishing this volume.

Burton was a unique town: railways everywhere. Stories abound, legends were borne. I have two favourites - the first I experienced. I arrived at the closed Blue Posts level crossing one Saturday morning, and after waiting a couple of minutes, suddenly a man on a cycle pedalled furiously across: the gates opened, and the road got back to normal. The crossing keeper didn't need to comment, his face and that of the man on the bike were a picture, both with a broad smile. The second story was also at the Blue Posts crossing, the gates closed to road traffic, a few minutes elapsed and they opened again. Someone asked the crossing keeper what had gone through: his response, 'The ghost train went through'.

Here's to the memory of Burton as a unique railway town.

H.N.Twells, OBE, Chesterfield, January 1997.

'Jubilee' 45663 JERVIS departs Burton on its journey south with the Down DEVONIAN on the 18th June 1957. B.W.L.Brooksbank.

INTRODUCTION

This volume is intended to complement my earlier book, Railways in Burton and the Trent Valley through 145 years, published by Trent Valley Publishing in 1984. Since then further research into official railway company records, in particular the old railway company Minute books at the Kew Public Record Office, has yielded much interesting detail about the railway scene in and around Burton upon Trent in the period since the 1830's. Further, new, photographic material, from many different sources, has enabled me to put together what will hopefully be a worthy companion to that earlier work.

The arrival of the railway was the start of an era which had a profound effect on the town. The effects were not only industrial and economical, but also the extent to which the network of railway lines serving the breweries developed until they threaded through the entire town, as evidenced by the number of level crossings which for over 100 years caused many a strong word for the delays occasioned to pedestrians and road vehicles.

This volume, therefore, provides further historical information and a range of interesting photographs from a variety of sources. If anyone has photographs of railway scenes or other historic material of the area covered by this book, I would appreciate hearing from them via the publishers.

CONTENTS

Midland Railway Distance Diagram (Burton on Trent 1915)

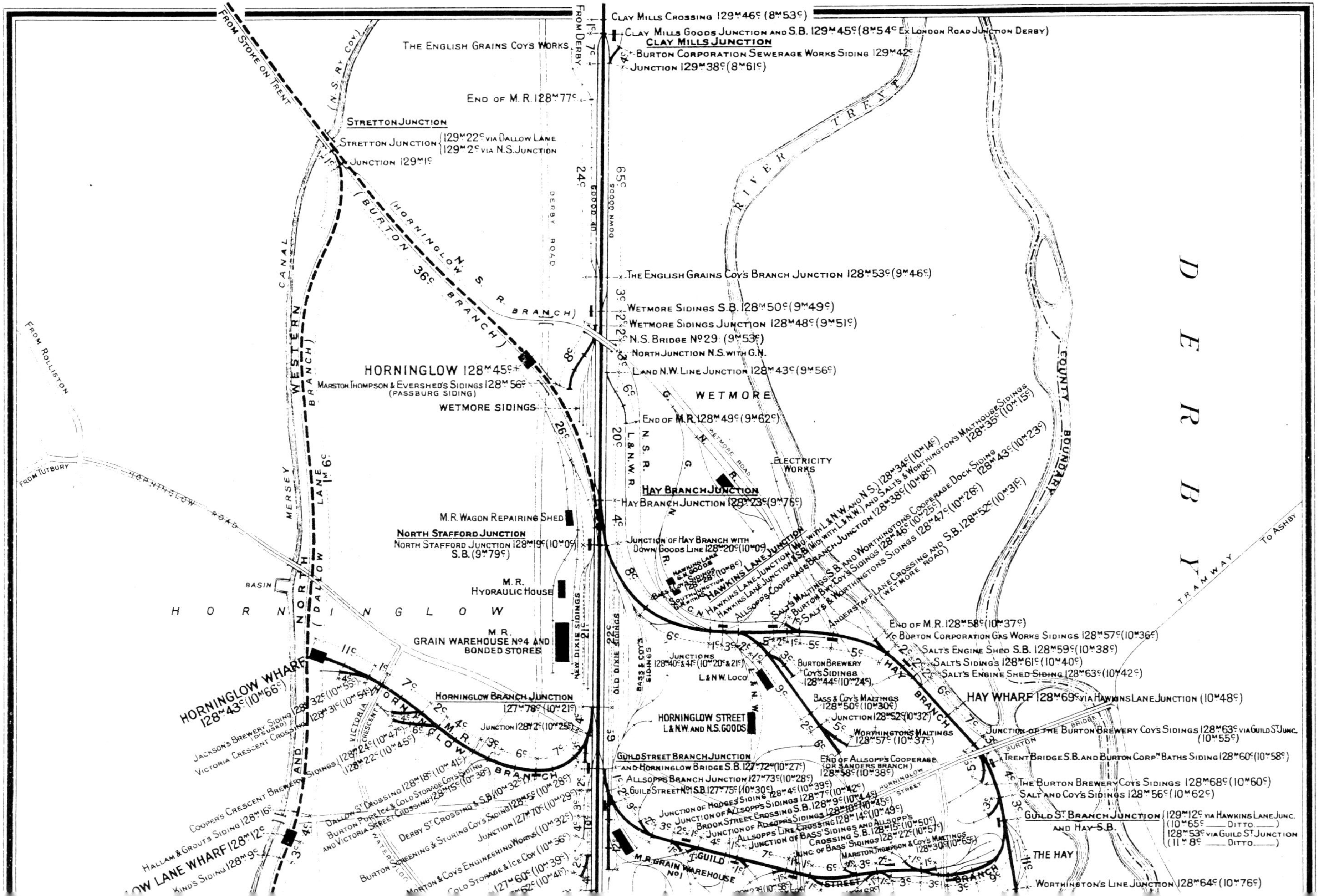

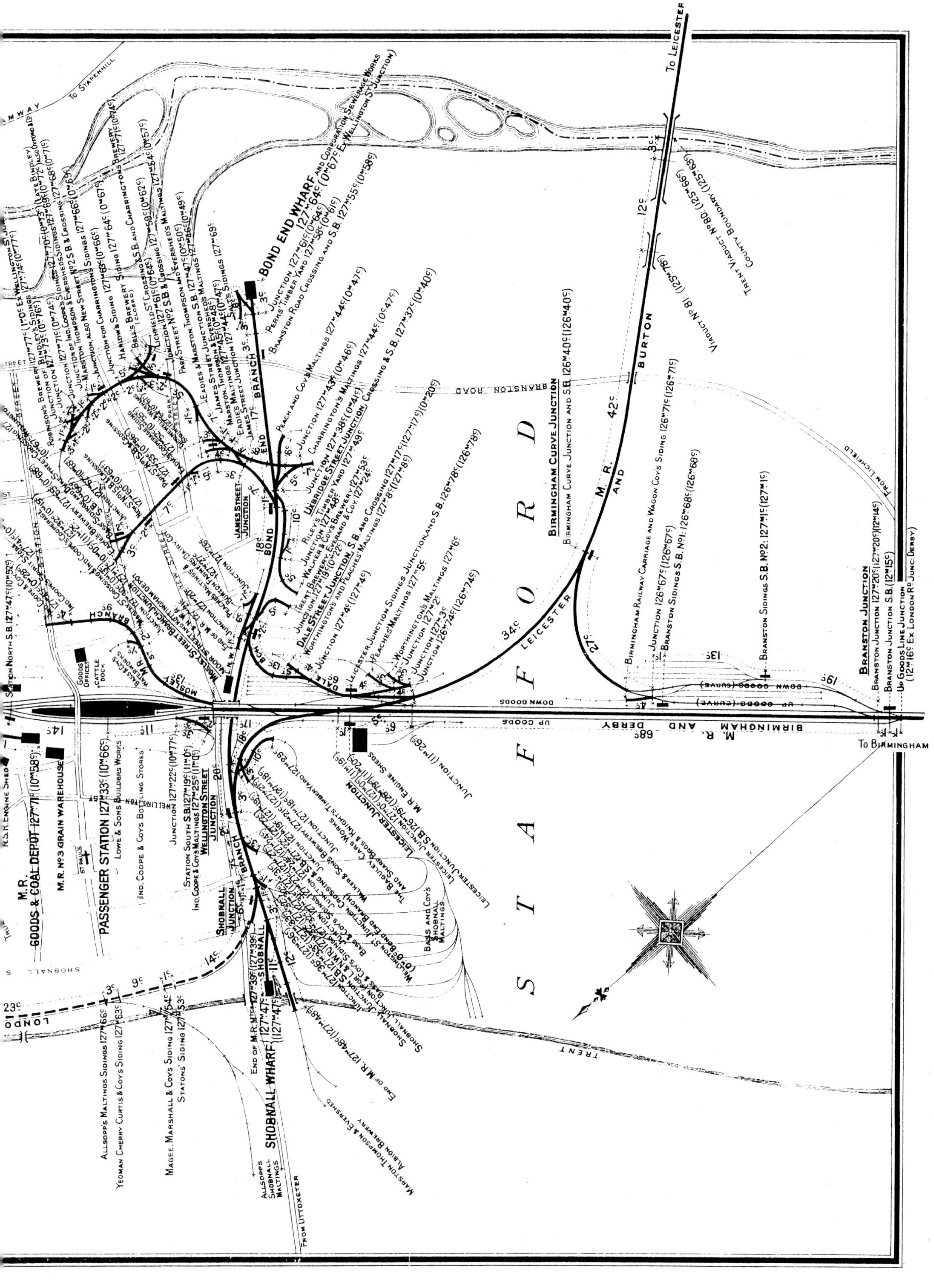
To Leicester
To Stapenhill
Bond End Wharf
Bond End Branch
James Street Junction
Uxbridge Street Junction
Dale Street Junction
Moor Street Junction
Mosley Street Branch
Leicester Junction
M.R. Engine Sheds
Wellington Street Junction
Shobnall Junction
Shobnall Wharf
Passenger Station 127m 33c (10m 66c)
M.R. Goods & Coal Depot 127m 7c (10m 58c)
M.R. No 3 Grain Warehouse
Birmingham Curve Junction
Branston Junction
Branston Road
M.R. and Burton
Leicester
M.R. and Derby
Birmingham
To Birmingham
From Lichfield
From Uttoxeter
Trent
Stafford
Down Goods
Up Goods
Marston, Thompson & Evershed Albion Brewery
Allsopps Shobnall Maltings
Bass and Coys Shobnall Maltings

BURTON UPON TRENT - RAILWAY TOWN EXTRAORDINAIRE

The East Staffordshire town of Burton upon Trent was already a noted brewery town by the time the first railway proposals for a route through the Trent valley were made.

The railway era was developing as plans were laid before Parliament, and George Stephenson was engaged to survey a route to link the London & Birmingham Railway with Derby to the north. The relatively flat terrain adjoining the River Trent made for easy construction with few problems. The movement of beer from Burton by canal and horse vehicle had attracted the attention of the railway-pioneering industrialists, and a railway connection from the London & Birmingham to Burton would provide an immediate source of beer traffic to London and return empties from the Capital, thus boosting the L&B revenue earning activities.

The Birmingham & Derby Junction Railway Company was formed on the 19th May 1836, and whilst George Stephenson was initially engaged as the Company's Engineer, his involvement with several other proposed railway construction projects led to him recommending his son, Robert, to take over as Engineer, and this change was agreed. The line was completed throughout some three years later on the 5th August 1839, with official opening one week later on the 12th.

The original proposal was for a connection with the London & Birmingham Railway at Stechford, three miles to the east of the L&B's Curzon Street terminus, to give access to Birmingham. A second link with the London & Birmingham line was established with a line running from the Birmingham & Derby at Whitacre to a junction with the L&B nine miles south of Curzon Street, at Hampton-in-Arden.

The route from Stechford towards Derby was generally a descending one and relatively flat as it came through Croxall from Tamworth and entered the low plains surrounding the River Trent. Whilst there were no major constructional problems, the low plains along the Trent Valley were liable to flooding and the trackbed was built up to several feet above the lowest areas. The route from Barton and Walton station towards Derby was straight for $5^1/_2$ miles, and remained so until the construction of the new island platform at Burton in 1883, albeit that this caused only a slight deviation from the otherwise straight course.

The southerly approach to Burton necessitated crossing the Burton Canal, and a drawbridge was installed to provide for the passage of both rail and canal traffic. An accident in 1846 led to the drawbridge being replaced by a permanent bridge over the canal, and the line for several hundred yards either side of the canal had to be raised to allow sufficient clearance for canal traffic. The 'hump' remains to this day a hundred or so yards to the south of the present station.

At this time minimal facilities existed alongside the main tracks, but these were set to be developed, as the town's breweries and other industries became heavily dependent on the railways. Such was the volume of traffic generated by breweries, that a network of railway lines became threaded through the town - a railway town without equal.

The opening of the Birmingham & Derby Junction Railway was a significant development in the first 'railway route to the North' and it was the first railway to arrive in Derby. Two further lines were being constructed, the **North Midland Railway** from Derby to Rotherham (opened 11th

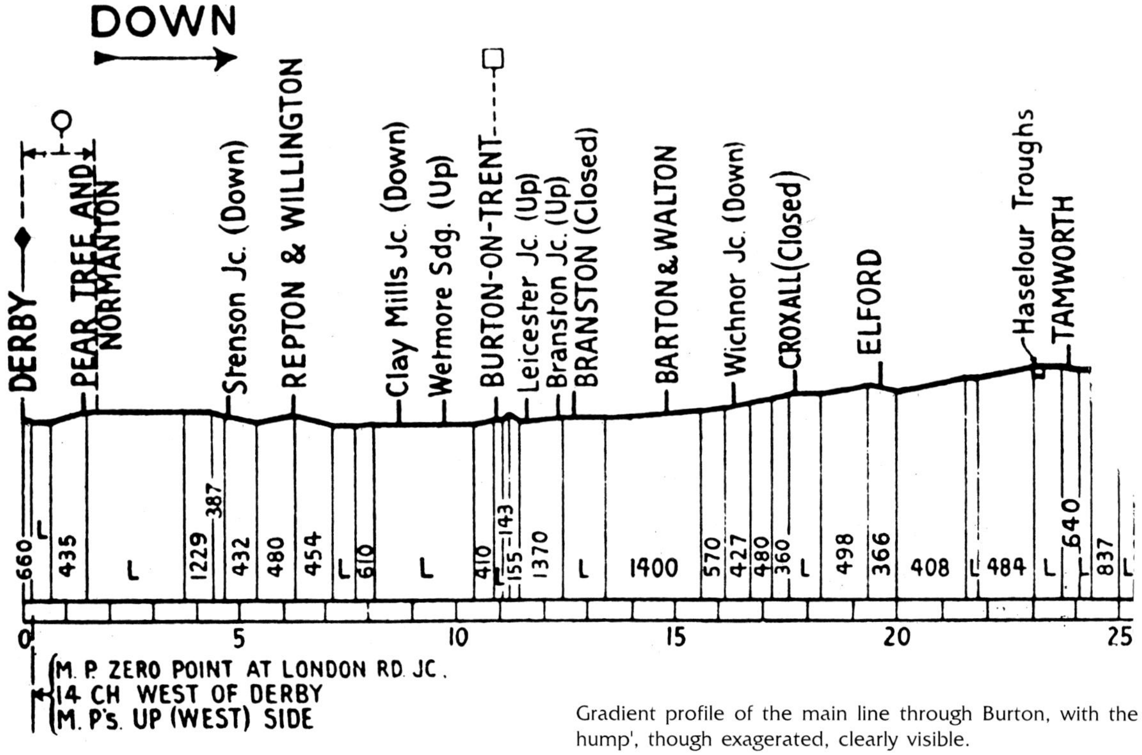

Gradient profile of the main line through Burton, with the 'canal hump', though exagerated, clearly visible.

This is an intriguing photograph. Crowds lining the Trent bridge can be seen in the hazy background, suggesting that the engine and three crew might be marooned on the Hay sidings, although the depth of water would appear to be no more than six inches above rail level, and therefore not sufficient to affect the engine. The photographer is probably on another engine or in a wagon, or possibly perched on the brick wall which seperated the sidings from the surrounding meadows. One of the hazards of siting a town on the flood plain of a river is one that Burtonians have to live with. G.Barnett collection

May 1840), and the **Midland Counties Railway** from Derby to Leicester and onto Rugby, to a junction with the London & Birmingham Railway (opened 30th June 1840). Thus, within a space of ten months, the Burton brewery companies gained easy transportation routes to many towns in the north and south, and two routes into London, and competition for their traffic was set to become intense.

The B&DJR was the initial carrier from Burton, either south to join directly with the London & Birmingham Railway at Hampton-in-Arden, or north to Derby for the Midland Counties route. Freight rates were cut for both routes, but the MCR route via Derby was the shorter of the two by $10^{3}/_{4}$miles. Whilst the brewers benefitted, the railway companies suffered cut-throat competition and came near to bankruptcy.

The first major amalgamation of railway companies came in 1844, with the formation of **The Midland Railway Company**. The Birmingham & Derby Junction, the North Midland, and the Midland Counties railways were brought together from 10th May 1844 and not surprisingly the headquarters was to be Derby.

The Midland Railway continued to develop its facilities within Burton to cope with the ever increasing traffic being generated by the breweries and the other industries, which were also growing, and by early 1884, the last and shortest of the eight Midland Branch lines through the town, the Dale Street Branch, was opened to traffic.

The Midland Railway era came to an end when the Company was merged with twenty seven other railway companies, to form the **London Midland & Scottish Railway Company** from the 1st January 1923. The LMS Railway continued to carry traffic to and from the town until it was subsumed into the nationalised **British Railways** from 1st January 1948.

The face of transportation was gradually changing in the years thereafter, and the 1960's period was to see a progressive rundown in rail traffic from the breweries, and the other industries, with the closure of the Midland branches through the town completed when the Shobnall Branch/ Shobnall Maltings Branch siding was closed on 31st October 1979.

Pages 8 & 9. **This 1950s aerial view of Burton encompasses virtually all of the town. Following the course of the meandering River Trent, on the right, the railway runs northwards from bottom left to top right. The line to Leicester curves away from the main line at bottom left opposite the ex-Midland engine sheds whilst the station sits in the middle of the conurbation. All the various branches and brewery sidings are visible snaking through the town.** Authors collection.

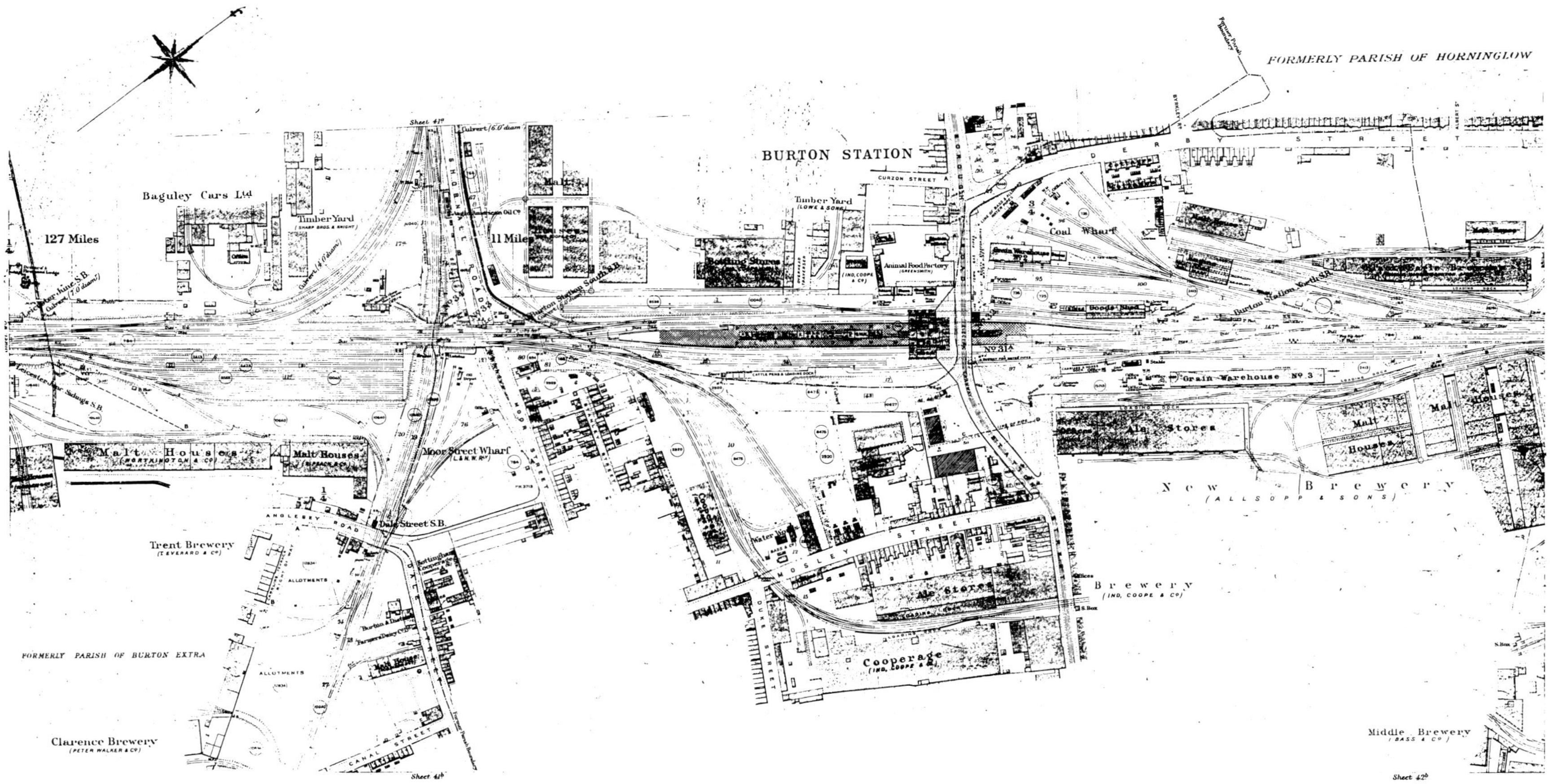

Fig 2. **Rating plan of the area around Burton (MR) station as surveyed in December 1922.**

BURTON UPON TRENT PASSENGER STATIONS

There have been four distinct station-periods since the arrival of the Birmingham & Derby Junction Railway in 1839. The first station 'came' with the railway in 1839. The line opened for traffic on 12th August 1839, but the station opening is quoted from the 8th December that year - this undoubtedly relates to the building itself being opened. It is probable that passengers used a temporary platform between these two dates, whilst construction work on the main platform and building was completed.

The earliest station building is believed to have been a hut adjacent to the level crossing which took Cat Street Lane (later to be renamed Station Street) across the lines, from which the crossing keeper operated, and from which tickets were issued and collected. A number of buildings were constructed as can be seen from the 1844 plan (fig.3), which shows the route of a proposed **Direct London & Manchester Railway**, crossing the Birmingham & Derby route, described as the B&D branch of the Midland Railway.

As traffic increased, further buildings were added to form the second station, principally a large two-storey building with canopy over the entrance. By 1847 the original hut had reverted to 'crossing keeper' use. A plan of 1847 depicted a proposed route for a **Grand Junction & Midland Union Railway**, from the Grand Junction Railway at Stafford, to the Midland Railway east of Derby. Whilst a another plan from the same year (fig.4) shows the extent of further developments.

With passenger and parcels traffic from the town continuing to increase, and increases in the number of trains, both passenger and freight passing through Burton, there was a growing bottleneck through the station. The original two lines - Up to Derby, Down to Birmingham - were insufficient. The platforms with facing buildings, goods sidings and engine sidings all outside the two running lines, left no room to increase the number of lines through the station. Proposals were therefore made to build a new, third, station some 7 chains (154 yards) to the south of the second station, and this opened on 29th April, 1883.

It was an altogether larger station, built on two levels. An island platform with substantial office, waiting and restaurant rooms were provided at rail level. The two fast lines, with an outside goods line in each direction overcame the through-rail traffic bottleneck. A new bridge for road traffic was provided over the railway, taking the same curved route from the end of Station Street, as the Cat Street Lane roadway and level crossing. Passenger access from the road was through booking office buildings situated on the crown of the bridge. Road vehicle access, at that time for horse-drawn carriages, was accommodated at the front of the station, with more than ample space for those awaiting the arrival of trains.

The third station fell victim to the British Railways modernisation plans, and a progressive reduction in the number of train passengers switching to buses and their own cars. The buildings on the bridge, and down the centre of the island platform, were demolished in 1970. The bridge remains, as does the cast-iron stairway between rail and road levels, monuments to the halcyon days of Burton's railways. The replacement buildings at both levels - the 'third' station-period - now forming the fourth station, are of totally modern and minimal facility. It is now one of only two stations between Birmingham and Derby, the other being at Tamworth. Principal services are South-west to North-east cross country operated by modern high-speed HST 125 Inter-City push pull units, with additional local services provided by two and three-car diesel sprinter trains, a far cry from the days when Burton was a major rail intersection of services. Gone are the passenger services to Tutbury, to Leicester, and to Lichfield and Walsall, although occasionally when trains are diverted via Lichfield to and from Birmingham, to allow engineering work on the Tamworth line, Lichfield once again appears on the passenger station menu card and in station announcements.

If the two stations at Horninglow are included, then the town has been served by a total of six stations.

From the earliest days of the railway, all decisions taken in the multitude of committees were meticulously minuted,

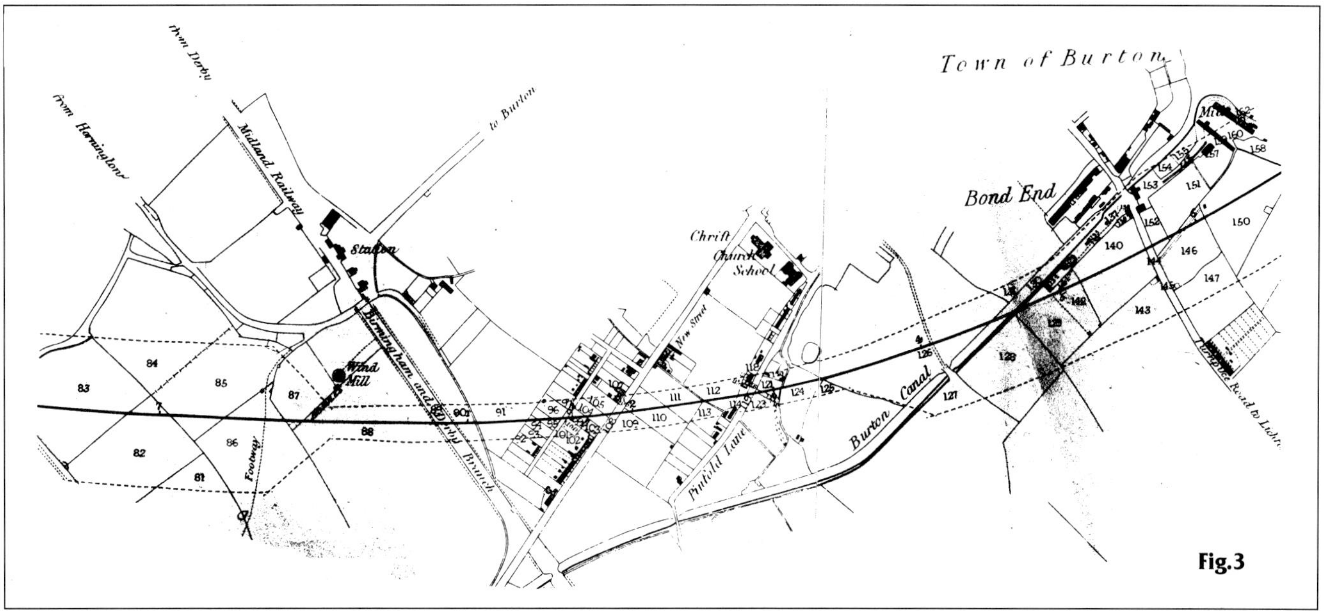

Fig.3

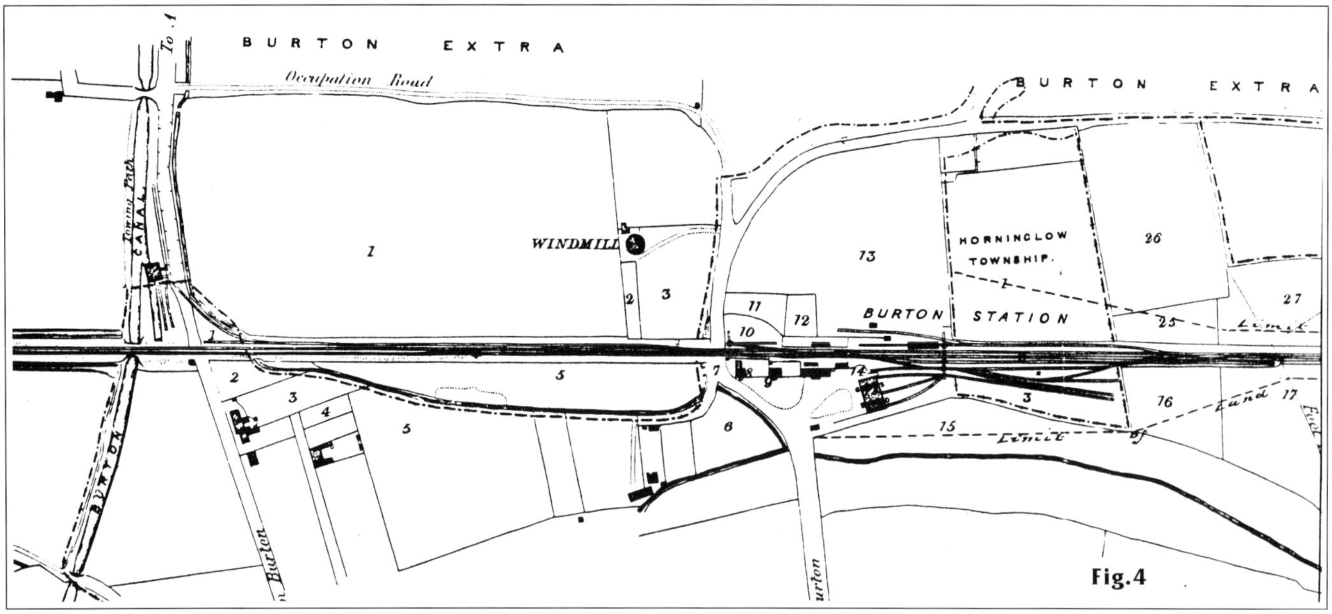

Fig.4

and the records of the Midland Railway Management, and Traffic Committees, have been researched for early references to the railways in the Burton area. There is much of interest in these old records, and a summary of the principal points is included in this section.

An early Midland Minute relating to Burton refers to the provision of a weighing machine, approved 2nd June 1845. An indication that a goods shed existed comes from a Minute of 1st July 1845, authorising repairs at a cost of £12. Similarly, 'another' crane was authorised on 5th August, whilst in November 1845, the need for an additional Waiting Room was discussed. It was decided at the December Management meeting that a lobby would be formed at the door of the General Waiting Room, and the omnibus (horse-drawn) and cab drivers would be excluded from this new Waiting Room. On the 17th February 1846, it was agreed a room over the water tank would be made into a Goods Office, but the work did not proceed immediately. In May 1850 this subject was again discussed with agreement to seek tenders. Yet more covered accommodation was authorised on 14th April 1846, when a shed, the length of six wagons, was to be erected and a 6 ton crane provided.

The Burton canal was still used in the 1840's for carrying goods to and from the Trent & Mersey Canal at Shobnall. The railway crossed the canal at a point south of the present station, alongside the old Moor Street road. A railway line was laid from the main line to the side of the canal, to serve a small warehouse for transit traffic.

On 21st September 1847, the purchase of additional land for the enlargement of Burton station was authorised and the need for a Refreshment Room is evidenced in a Minute of 3rd July 1849, which instructed the Company Secretary to apply for the necessary licence. A Minute of 23rd April 1850 reports tenders for construction of two sets of 'privies' (earth toilets), work which proceeded at a cost of £22.13.6d.

Platform repairs on the east side of the railway - the Birmingham platform - were authorised on 28th May 1850. Repairs to the south end of the platform were to be done with asphalt and the remainder of the platform was to be supported with old stone blocks. However, as a result of further

(left) **The station entrance approached from the town end, showing the very substantial and attractive structure of the 1883 buildings on the bridge. The posters advertise return trips to Glasgow £6.8s., Edinburgh £6.6s., Blackpool £2.10s., and a number of other attractive fare deals in late 1969.** Author

(opposite) **The station approach from the Borough Road end of the town shown here in September 1962.** B.W.L.Brooksbank

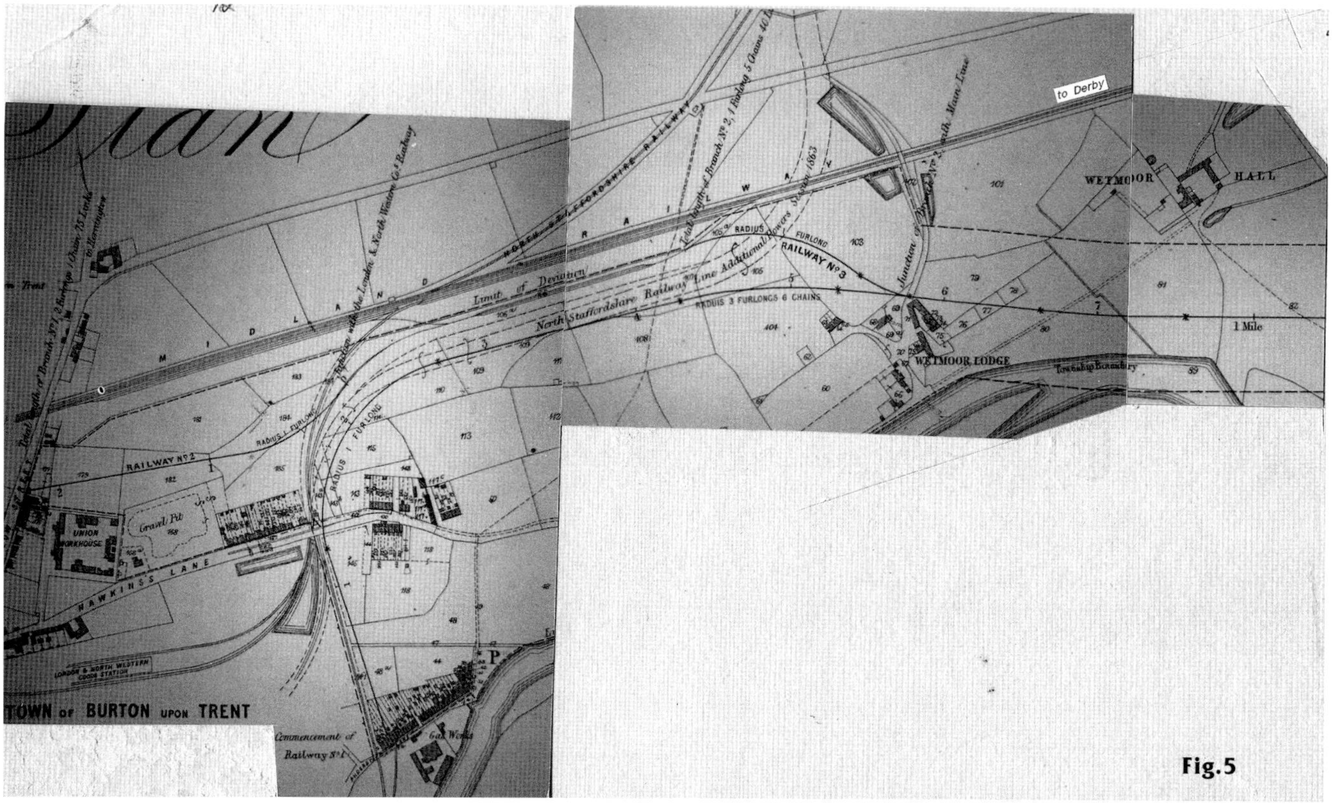

Fig.5

discussion two months later, it was decided that the whole of the original wooden platform was to be replaced with asphalt.

An indication that goods traffic between the railway and canal was reducing comes from a discussion on 11th June 1850, when it was decided the Goods Shed at the side of the canal should be dismantled and re-located at the Burton goods yard. The need for a new Cheese warehouse was discussed in 1851 and evidence of increasing rail traffic, comes from a further discussion in July 1852 when it was proposed that the planned size of the Cheese warehouse should be increased by one half of the original size. This was opened in 1854. In June 1856, Management sought a return to show what quantity cheese had been stored in the new warehouse during the previous twelve months, showing if possible, the quantities which had been conveyed to and from the warehouse in road carts or wagons, from that which had been conveyed by the railway. Reference to further alterations at the station is made in a Minute of 14th July 1852, but no details are recorded.

The Station Refreshment Rooms had been let in 1849 on a three year lease, and the tenant gave notice of leaving at the end of 1852. The tenancy was advertised and it was let to a Mr C.Lees for three years at a rental of £110 per annum. He appears to have remained as tenant for a long period. The last lease extension referred to in the Management Committee

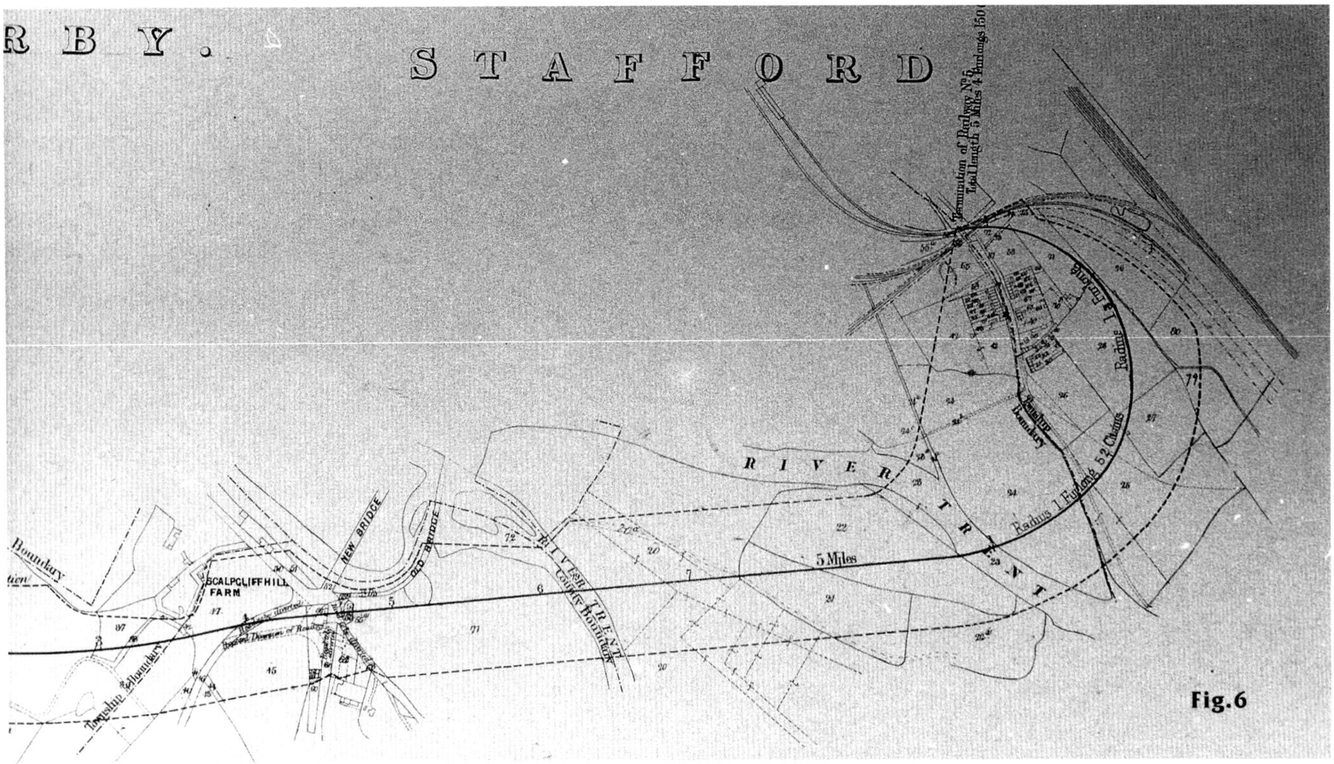

Fig.6

Minutes was granted for three years from January 1865. Thereafter, all matters relating to the Midland Railway's Refreshment Rooms were transferred to a Midland Hotels Committee sometime between 1864 and 1867.

It would appear that the first footbridge over the railway was ordered on 2nd September 1856, at a cost of £243, and set in a line with an existing footpath. This may well be the iron bridge just north of the station. Uneven stone sets (more commonly known as cobblestones) required attention in late 1857, and re-setting was authorised, the terms being at 6d per yard if the company provided the necessary gravel, or 10d per yard if the contractor found the gravel. A Yeast Dock for the station yard was authorised in February 1858.

The Deputy Coroner for Burton wrote to the Midland Railway Company in September 1859 pointing out that, "as a consequence of a fatal accident lately at the station, it was a necessity to shift the pillars on the Platform". The Management Committee received a report from the Traffic Committee stating the pillars should be removed altogether, and the matter referred to the Company's Engineer. Whether they were removed is perhaps in doubt, for in November 1862, there is reference to the "columns on the passenger platforms".

The first reference to the provision of horse stables comes in a Minute of 15th May 1860, when it was decided that Messrs Thompson & Fryer's tender for the construction of stables for six horses and a loose box should be accepted. This gives a clear indication of the introduction of railway-owned cartage services by the Midland, as this is the first Minute referring to the construction of the Company's own stables. In addition to Burton, stables were also authorised in the same Minute at seven other stations, with a further twelve authorised on the 3rd July 1860.

Burton station from the roadbridge in September 1962. This view is in the direction of Leicester Junction and the afternoon sun casts a gentle light over the scene. The architectural style of the building is more akin to those stations found in northern mainland Europe. Whatever one's ideas about the style, it was certainly an attractive building and would surely have got 'listed' status had it still been standing today. B.W.L.Brooksbank.

A view of platform 4 with the bookstall adorned with posters and advertising material. W.H.Smith's bookstall was later moved to face the bottom of the steps, as seen in the following view. The viewing balcony at the rear of the road-level buildings is seen in this summer view. F.W.Shuttleworth collection

An interesting report to the Management meeting on 5th November, 1861, refers to Messrs Allsopp sinking a monster well, which had caused the wells supplying the station to become dry. The pure water supplies which are the principal constituent of the world-renowned beer, are of course drawn through a series of wells from an artesian well bed lying beneath the town.

On 6th January 1863, it was ordered that a Porters Room be provided at the station to hold a boiler for feet warmers - a luxury service provided for passengers in unheated carriages.

The Station Master was invited in March 1863 to occupy the company's house near to Horninglow Bridge, which may have been the first Horninglow station which was shown on a plan of c.1860.

A further indication of the increasing goods traffic comes with a discussion in November 1865, when it was agreed that "two of the bays in the goods warehouse should be covered over to provide more platform accommodation".

By August 1870, the original wooden station footbridge, between the platforms, was considered unsafe, and tenders were invited for constructing a new wrought iron lattice girder bridge in its place. One month later a price of £258 was accepted.

A new station for the town appears to have been discussed for the first time early in 1873. The cost was stated to be £39,635 and plans were ordered to be drawn up. Authorisation to purchase additional land for the enlargement of the station was given on 2nd December 1873 and a further quantity of land was to be leased. Even though plans had been drawn for the replacement of the station, alterations to the Refreshment Rooms at the second station were approved in December 1877. The new station plans were discussed at virtually every Management Committee meeting in 1879, and it was resolved to seek tenders. In 1881 contracts were let for the new station, a new bridge over the line, new trackwork and signalling, at a total cost of £69,000. Later costs to be added were for a hoist between road and platform, gas lamps on the platforms and around the station entrance. The new station, Burton's third, was opened from 29th April 1883. The facilities provided were on a grand scale, and were destined to serve the town and its rail passengers well for eighty-eight years, until demolition in 1971.

The platform length was reduced by removing the lengths of platform which had fronted the Bay platforms at either end of the station. The fourth station consists a single waiting room and toilet building, with canopy, at platform level whilst there is a small booking office at road level - a far cry from the 1883 station facilities.

A number of further railway route proposals were made, which if they had materialised, would have brought further development to the Burton area.

The Burton & Nottingham Railway and **The London & North Western & Midland Counties Coalfields Railway** proposals, both of 1865, would have approached the town from the north and eastern sides respectively, both linking with the existing lines in the Dixey area of the town. The proposed Burton & Nottingham Railway route (fig.5) came in from the Ingleby and Repton side, crossing relatively low-lying land prone to flooding, which would have necessitated embankments along virtually the entire route from Nottingham. The L&NWR & Midland Counties Coalfields Railway (see fig.6) would have come in from a junction proposed at Hartshorne in South Derbyshire. Tunnels would have been necessary on the route proposed, and it would have crossed the River Trent close to the point where the Swan Hotel and present Trent Bridge were subsequently built.

(above) **The Birmingham platform, No 4, in 1953. W.H.Smith's bookstall is now in its new position facing the intending travellers as they descend the stairway, although a scan of the departure indicator would probably take priority. The posters make interesting reading, even for 1953 - 'Health for all, HOW TO CURE HEADACHES', whilst another poster proclaims 'BRITISH INTERPLANETARY PLANS' published in the Picture Post magazine.** Author's collection

(middle) **Fine building detail can be seen in this platform view, taken in the late LMS period. The Refreshment Room remained open until the late 1960's. Note the iron grills providing ventilation to cellars beneath platform level.** V.R.Anderson

(left) **The south-end Bay platform 3, with a number of rail-tour enthusiasts taking a look at the surroundings on 14th October, 1962. This bay was used by trains starting their journeys from Burton, for Lichfield, Walsall and Wolverhampton, and also the Leicester line. The sidings on the left, adjacent to the Ind Coope & Allsopp bottling plant, were used from the late 1940's for the storage of surplus old MR and LMS kitchen, dining and sleeping carriages.** H.B.Oliver

The north-end Bay platform, No. 2, with the 'Tutbury Jenny' push-pull service awaiting departure in August 1953. Note the gas lamps have the later style of top fitting, with the metal disc above the mantle globe, to reduce the upwards and sidewards glow in the dark, introduced as a war-time measure. G.A.Yeomans

The sad end of the quite majestic 1883 buildings, which had graced the Burton skyline, seen here on 20th June 1971. New steel posts and girders stand in place on the right, to support a new short canopy at the foot of the stairway. M.A.King

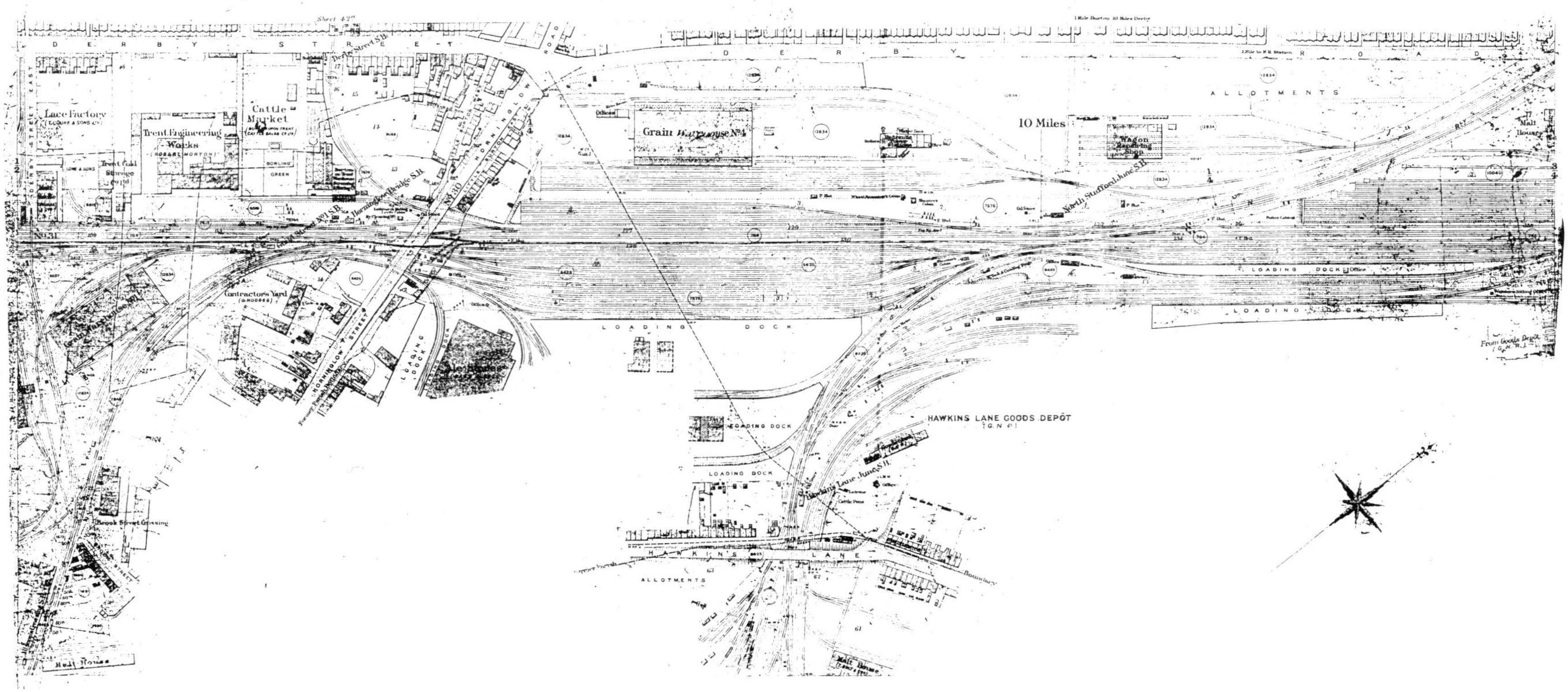

Fig. 7. **Rating plan of the area north of the MR station to North Stafford Junction. (December 1922)**

THE MAIN-LINE THROUGH BURTON

This is the route of the original Birmingham & Derby Junction Railway. It was completed on 5th August 1839, and opened to traffic one week later. It was immediately an integral part of the first south-north rail link between London and Leeds and York, and later to Darlington in the north-east, carrying the first through-carriage services between different railway companies along this route. By 1846 it was also part of a direct route from the north, to Gloucester and Bristol via Birmingham.

Measured from the '0' milepost at the south end of Derby station, milepost 11 was adjacent to the Moor Street level crossing at the south end of Burton station, and it was a further 13 miles to Tamworth High Level station. The stations, with opening and closing dates are laid out in the table below.

From Derby:-	Opened	Closed
WILLINGTON	12/8/1939	—
became **WILLINGTON & REPTON** from 1/10/1855	—	—
then **REPTON & WILLINGTON** from 1/5/1877	—	—
then **WILLINGTON for REPTON** from 1/10/1889	—	—
then **REPTON & WILLINGTON** in use by 12/1898	—	4/3/1968
HORNINGLOW	(a)	?
BURTON (first station)	8/12/1839	—
BURTON (larger second station)	by 1847	—
BURTON (third station)	29/4/1883	—
BURTON (fourth station)	from 1971	remains in use.
BRANSTON	1/10/1889	22/9/1930
BARTON & WALTON	12/8/1839	5/8/1958
WICHNOR JUNCTION	2/4/1855	1/8/1856

Notes.
(a) First station marked on map C.1860 by Horninglow Bridge/Derby Road Junction.
Horninglow station on North Staffs - Tutbury line - opened as Burton Horninglow from 1 August, 1883, and was described as the second station at Horninglow.

were all replaced by bridges over the railway, except for Moor Street, where the roadway was taken beneath the railway. From Clay Mills Junction, through to Branston, the route was four tracks wide and three tracks between Branston and Barton & Walton. Such was the volume of traffic using the line, that freight and coal trains were often nose-to-tail back from Barton, awaiting a path between fast traffic on the main line. The sidings at Wichnor Junction were used for splitting and re-assembling trains, and it is somewhat surprising that the Midland did not instal additional slow lines between Barton and Wichnor, a distance little more than one mile. Although the route lay along the lowlands bordering on the River Trent, which were prone to flooding, the tracks were carried on embankments. Whilst the streets of the town near to the Burton station are known to have been flooded on several occasions, no records have been found to indicate that the main-line track-bed was ever covered in floodwater.

From the south end of Burton station it was possible to sight a train, albeit a 'blip', as it came north onto the straight section at Barton, some four miles distant.

The journey between Burton and Derby took Birmingham & Derby Junction Railway trains 35 minutes, for the eleven mile stretch, despite the line being relatively level throughout. With the development of larger locomotives the time was soon halved by the Midland to around 17 minutes.

South of Burton, there was a rising gradient from Barton & Walton to Tamworth and the 13 miles stretch took around 21 minutes, with 18 minutes for Tamworth - Burton, mostly on a descending gradient.

The route carried heavy traffic, and much of it was loaded coal and mineral trains from Toton marshalling yards near Nottingham, to and from the Birmingham area, as well as brewery trains into and out of Burton with a variety of fast 'fitted' trains passing through Burton also. Branston station, adjacent to the old A38 turnpike road bridge, was the last main-line station to open in 1889, and the first to close, in September 1930. The platforms however, remained in situ until the mid-1960's.

When the line was first built there were level crossings at Barton & Walton, most probably Branston for the first few years, Moor Street crossing, and as Wetmore Road crossed the railway lines on the northern boundary of the town. They

A late afternoon view at the south-end of platform 4, with one of the 0.F class, 0-4-0 saddle tanks ready to move off, whilst the two enginemen are on their way from the sheds off duty.

A rather tranquil morning scene at the north-end, with class 2F 58186, a long-time Burton engine, trundling a pair of coal wagons past the station, for setting back into the coal yard behind the building on the right. E.Woods

'Jubilee' 45557 NEW BRUNSWICK, at the head of a southbound fitted freight on 30th May 1964. The weeds begin to take over the No.2 Bay platform, four years after the withdrawal of the 'Tutbury Jenny' service. The engine is seen at the point where the second station building stood prior to 1883. Paul A.Forbes

A visitor from the Eastern Region, B1 class 61002, IMPALA, at the head of a northbound empty mineral wagon train on 6th March, 1965. The Midland wooden signal gantry is seen framing the engine, with the Burton Station North signal box beyond. The clouds of steam behind the signal box emanate from an engine in the coal yard sidings. Paul A.Forbes

Former Crosti boilered BR 9F 2-10-0 No.92027 takes the Up Goods line past the station on 30th May 1964. Paul A.Forbes.

This is a splendid view of the Truman's private siding, adjoining the main running lines, and the sidings which originally served the North Staffs Railway engine shed - located in the yard to the left prior to 1927. The notice board, prohibits the entry of 6-wheeled engines into Truman's sidings. Note the general clutter in this 1954 view taken from the iron footbridge north of the station. Burton Station North signal box is seen on the extreme left. Patrick Webb

This view is also from the iron footbridge, but it shows the station buildings in the left background, and the Derby Street yard and former North Staffs sidings adjoining Truman's brewery. Type 4 diesel electric D186 is at the head of Toton-bound rake of mineral empties, circa 1969. A.O.Wynn

(right) **Brewery warehouses and sidings dominated the area to the north of the station on the east side of the main-line. In this view on the left, is one of Ind Coope & Allsopp's grain warehouses, and in the background, their Head Office building. The smaller building behind the three carriages is the former MR No.2 Grain warehouse. 9F 2-10-0 92167, one of three in the class fitted with a mechanical stoker, heads the 16.48 Water Orton - Carlisle express freight. A Saltley shed working, it was the longest engineman's freight turn on British Railways.** Patrick Webb

(middle) **A Tinsley-Severn Tunnel Junction freight heading south towards Burton station, having just passed beneath the Horninglow Road bridge, with a Class 45 the train engine. Horninglow Bridge signal box is seen to the right of the train. Weeds are beginning to take over the little-used sidings on the right in this 1970 view.** A.O.Wynn

(bottom) **The 'Tutbury Jenny' push-pull service with the driver-trailer leading, returning to Burton. Two through carriages from a North Wales - Derby train, have been added to the 'Jenny' service at Tutbury and are seen behind the engine in this view. The building on the right is the former Midland Railway No.1 Grain warehouse. The Midland's Guild Street branch was behind this warehouse. Large numbers of old MR covered vans were used by Bass & Co, and here several stand awaiting further use. They were light grey, and as seen here, carried the Bass Red Triangle, British Trade Mark No. 1.** Patrick Webb

(above) **The view south from the Horninglow Road bridge, 10th June, 1969. At left is the commencement of the Guild Street branch on the left, the entrance to the No.1 warehouse and Ind Coope's sidings to the left of the Horninglow Bridge signal box. On the right of the main line are seen the sidings to Morton & Co. Engineering works, and the Trent Cold Storage & Ice Company's cold store. Truman's brewery dominates the skyline. Behind the iron footbridge, Burton station can just be discerned.** M.A.King

(middle) **The sidings adjoining the ex-MR No.4 warehouse (in the background) and to the west of the main-line, were known as the 'New Dixie sidings'. The 'merry-go-round' (MGR) wagon maintenance depot seen here in August 1979 was built in the mid-1970's for the repair of the large capacity coal wagons. 08623 goes about its chores with little effort.** A.O.Wynn

(left) **Wetmore sidings were north of Dixie, and here class 4F 0-6-0 44245 awaits the off, with a northbound freight. A 3F 0-6-0 is seen in the down yard on the left.** R.C.Riley

Wetmore Sidings signal box, a replacement box installed in June 1949, with the Wetmore Road bridge in the background. 0-6-0T 47643, one of the Glasgow Beardmore-built LMS tank engines of 1929, is shunting the Up yard on 31st May 1966. Paul A.Forbes

Eastern Region K1 2-6-0 62012 heads a morning steel train southbound on the slow line past Wetmore Sidings signal box on 16th October 1965. Paul A.Forbes

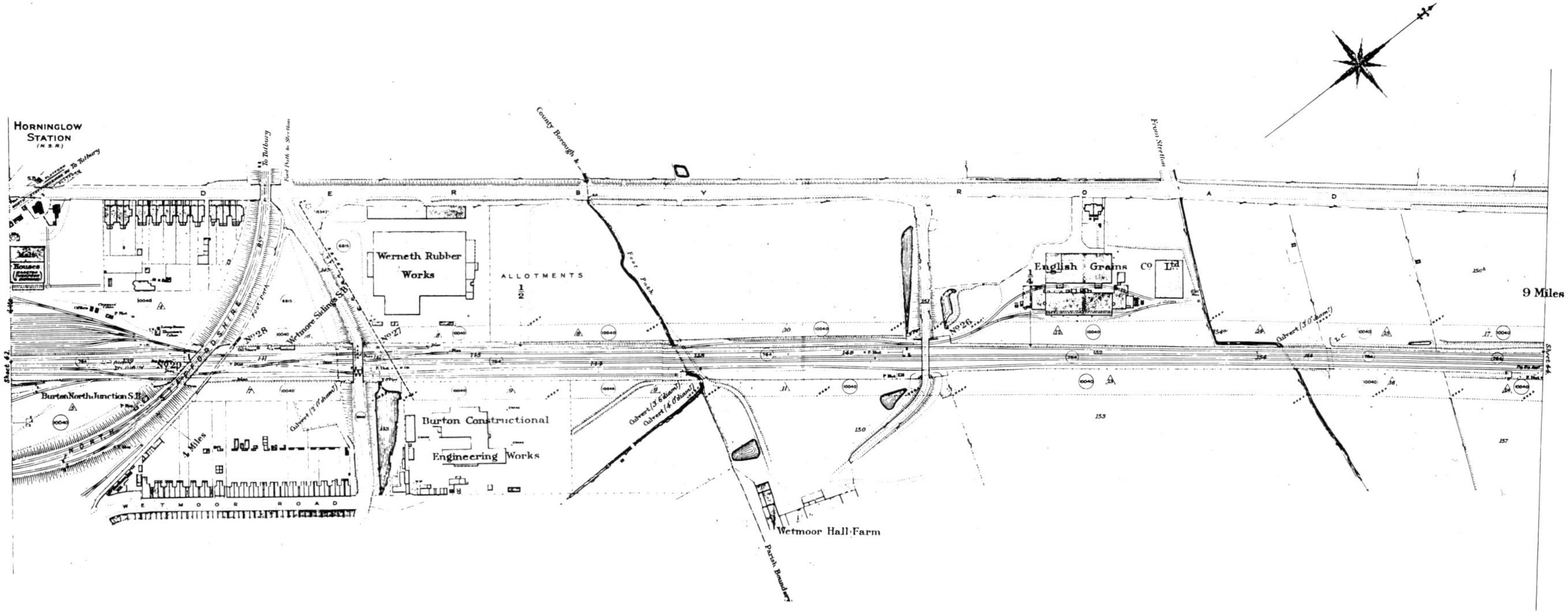

Fig.8. **Rating plan of the main line north of Wetmore sidings (December 1922)**

Burton was of course 'Garratt country' for nearly thirty years. Though none were ever allocated to the Burton shed, they were daily performers through the town on the long coal trains to Birmingham and beyond. Here Beyer-Garratt 47995 with a Bromford (Birmingham) - Toton empty wagon train, approaches Clay Mills Junction in June 1956, a year before it was withdrawn from traffic. Clay Mills Junction was the northern end of the four-track section through Burton, the 'junction' being no more than four lines merging into the two fast lines. Patrick Webb

0-6-0T 47485 collects wagons of spent-grain from the English Grains' private siding at Clay Mills, in the 1950's, and interestingly, the first wagon is a Maltby Colliery 9-plank private owner coal wagon. The second wagon is also in private owner livery, unfortunately not identifiable. The limit of railway company maintenance responsibility was at the point where the gate on the far left, closed to the post in the foreground. Patrick Webb

(left) **REPTON & WILLINGTON - ALIGHT FOR REPTON SCHOOL - proclaims the station nameboard on the down platform. One of the original Birmingham & Derby Junction Railway stations, it was located in the centre of Willington village, on a high embankment and, during its lifetime, had a number of name re-arrangements. Repton village was a mile or so to the east. A 3F 0-6-0 No.43826 is heading a south-bound mineral train on 15th April 1957.** M.A.King

(middle, left) **Taking the motor car as a guide, this view of Repton & Willington station would appear to be just prior to the First World War, perhaps 1912 or thereabouts. The horse-drawn bus is awaiting the next arrival, most probably providing a service to Repton village. The station staff and villagers pose for the cameraman.** Lens of Sutton

(opposite, top) **The Up-side buildings in the later Midland period. The second building on the left has been added after the previous photograph was taken. The nearer building may have been the first one installed, simply as a ticket issuing hut. The larger third, and the fourth structure appear to be from much the same period, whilst the second structure, a waiting shelter is the last one built.** Author's collection

(opposite, bottom) **Former Midland Johnson 3F 0-6-0, 3656, heads a mixed freight south on the stretch of line which runs alongside the Trent & Mersey Canal, which was once owned by the North Staffordshire Railway Company. When this photograph was taken on 20th May 1933, the canal was in the ownership of the London Midland & Scottish Railway Company. The end of the train is just passing the Stenson Junction signal box in the distance. This was one of the Johnson 0-6-0 engines built with a class 2 boiler, and later changed for a higher-rated class 3 boiler. Note the very tidy track-bed and the sand box.** E.R.Morten

(left) **The Willington Station signal box which stood at the Derby end of the station. This Midland box was installed in 1892 and closed seventy-seven years later, on 29th June 1969. This view was taken on 5th April 1969, a few weeks before closure and removal.** M.A.King

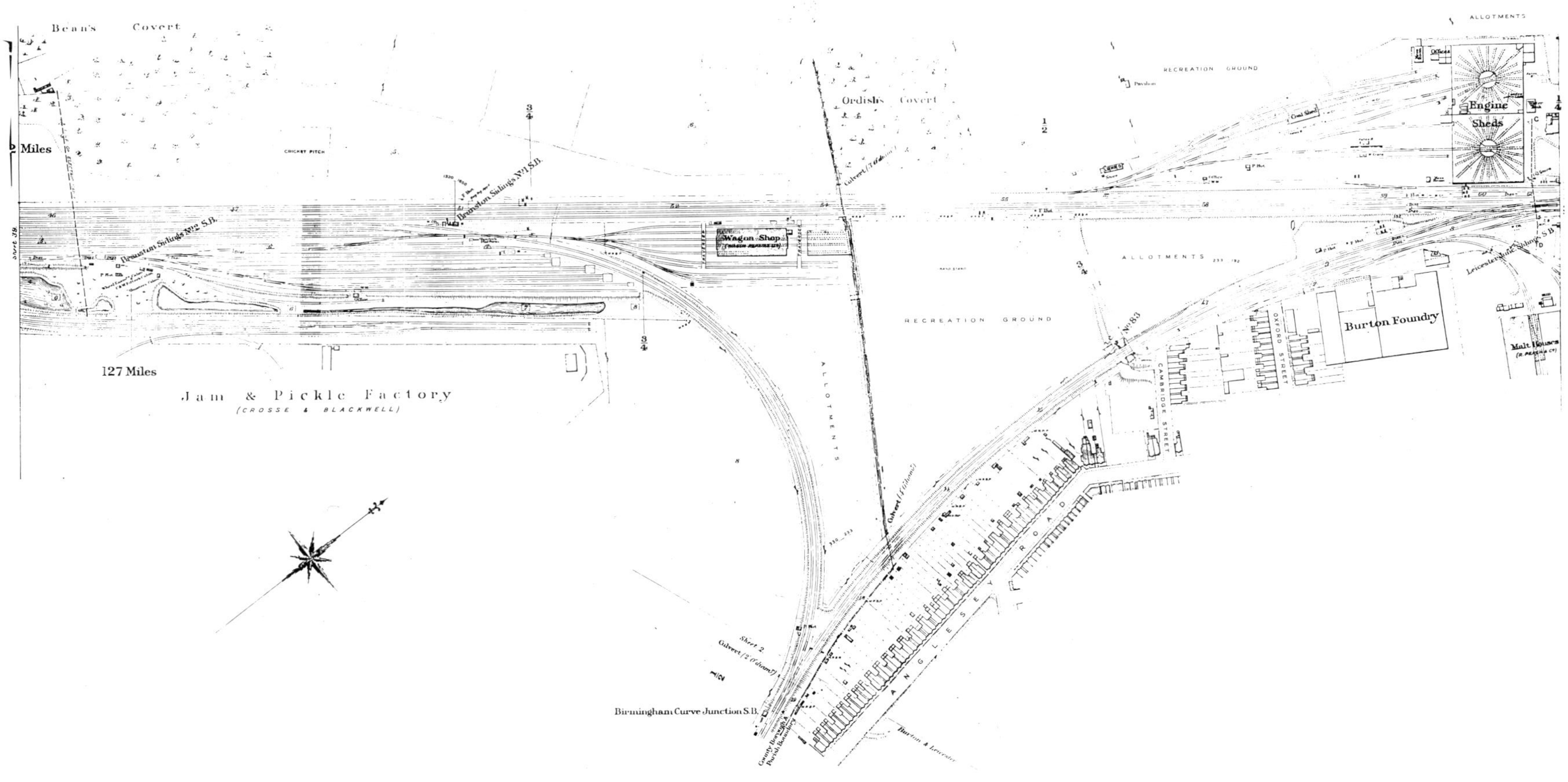

Fig.9. **Rating plan of main line south of Burton station to Branston sidings (Decemebr 1922)**

(right) **LMS 5182, one of the 1935 batch of Armstrong Whitworth 'Black 5' 4-6-0's leaves Burton for Bristol on the 17th September 1938. The Midland Railway wooden signal gantry was replaced by the tubular post signals shown in the previous two pictures.** E.R.Morten

'Jubilee' 45675 HARDY heads the 11.53 a.m. York-Bristol express out of Burton, towards Moor Street level crossing, on the 11th April 1965. The 'Jubilees' were the mainstay of the principal expresses on the route but by the date of this photograph diesels in the form of the 'Peaks' were gradually taking over their work. Paul A.Forbes.

Burton Station South signal box, exactly eleven miles from the '0' milepost at the south end of Derby station. The gates to the Moor Street level crossing are seen here, but the sleeper roadway across the tracks is no longer complete, and therefore the crossing was out of use when this view was taken on the 5th April, 1969. The '11' milepost can be seen on the left hand edge of the signal box. The 'hump', created in 1847 when the tracks were raised to give clearance to traffic on the Burton Canal, which passed beneath the railway, can be seen in this view. The tracks were raised over a quarter mile length to give several feet of additional clearance. The canal was later purchased by the Midland Railway company and drained, and it thereafter formed the track-bed of the two Midland branches which linked Bond End and Shobnall. A draw-bridge had originally been provided to take the railway tracks over the canal, but on the morning of 31st October 1846, in heavy fog conditions, an approaching train did not see the signal that the drawbridge was raised for canal traffic, and ploughed on and into the canal. That incident led to the installation of a permanent bridge to replace the drawbridge, and it is seen immediately beneath the signal gantry. M.A.King

One of the re-built 'Jubilee' 4-6-0 class engines, 45735 COMET relegated to fast freight duties, passing over the Moor Street level crossing heading south to Birmingham with a train of Carflats. The re-built engines were distinguished by the addition of 'Royal Scot' type smoke deflectors. The Moor Street crossing, with four, seven-panelled gates, was one of the widest crossing locations on the former Midland Railway. R.Newman

Three 4F 0-6-0's, 44091, 43995 and 43990, plus Beyer-Garratt 47986, pass Burton en-route from Washwood Heath, Birmingham, to Toton in 1954, having worked trains from Toton to Birmingham the previous day. Patrick Webb

This view shows the Leicester line junction 30th May 1960, with 0-4-0T 41536 heading south on the slow line, pushing a short train of vans. The signal gantries protecting the junction are seen to good effect. The signal box on the right is the Leicester Junction (Burton) box, whilst the one seen beneath the gantry, is the Leicester Junction Sidings Junction box, a small box controlling the entrance to the Dale Street Branch, and the Worthington's and Peaches Maltings private sidings. Note the shunter's pole at the front of the engine. R.C.Riley

The Leicester Junction (Burton) signal box with the Sharp Bros & Knight Ltd. timber stores behind. This was the fourth signal box on this site, dating from 1902, and it closed on the 15th June 1969. M.A.King

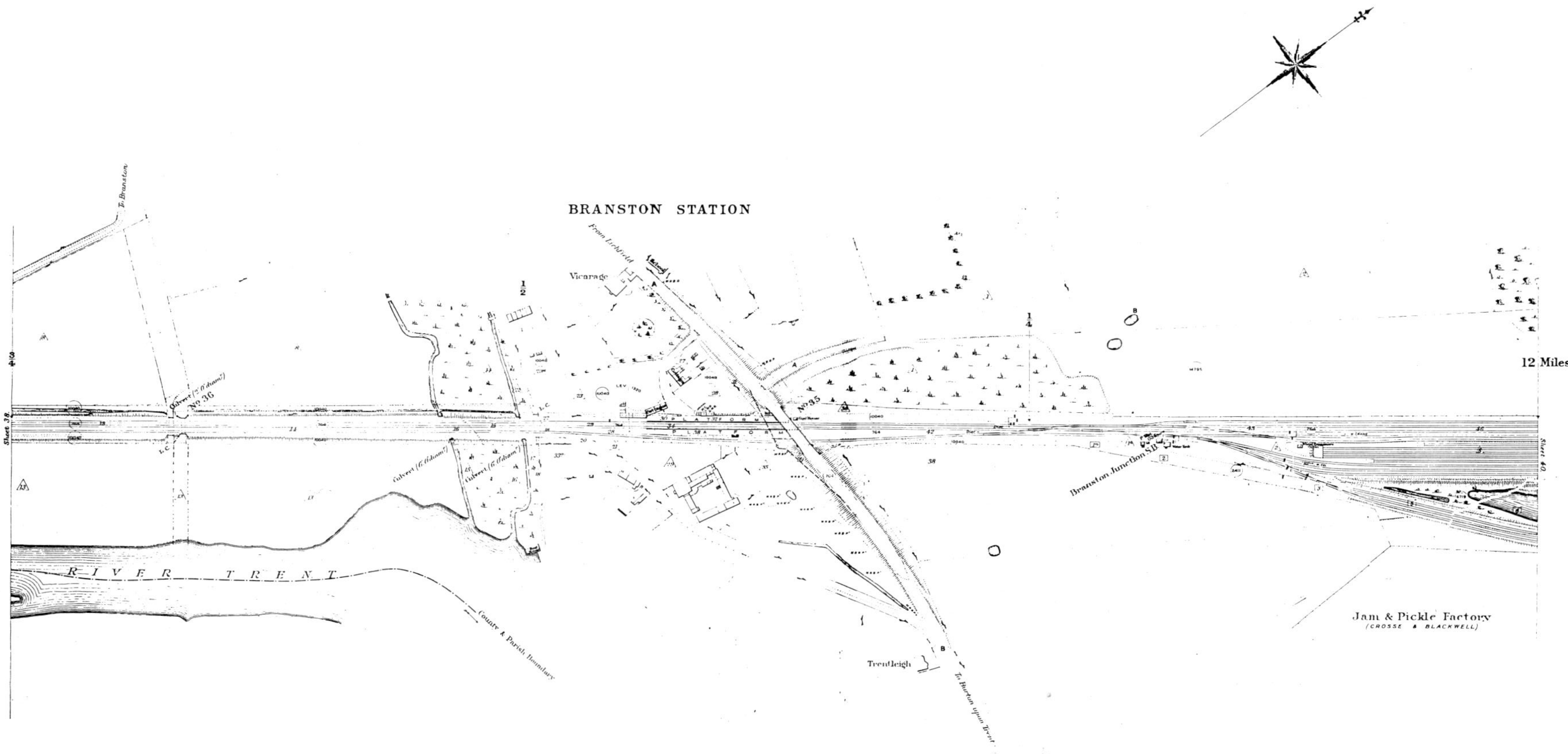

Fig. 10. **Midland Railway Rating plan of area around Branston station (October 1922)**

After passing Leicester Junction, and approaching Branston, there were sidings which served the Royal Ordnance Factory at Branston. In addition, access to the Leicester line could be gained through a tightly curved connection known as the Birmingham curve. The Branston Junction signal box controlled access to this connection, and to the sidings, and adjacent private wagon works owned by the Birmingham Carriage & Wagon Co. Ltd., which were located in the triangle of lines - mainline-Leicester line- Birmingham curve. This view dates from 13th August 1963. M.A.King

This is the only view of Branston station known to the author. The booking office is seen at roadway level, at the head of a stairway to the platform, and passengers had to cross the road bridge to gain access to the Down platform on which the photographer is standing. The period is c.1907, and a Midland train is arriving. Branston station was a late arrival, opening on the 1st October 1889, and closing on the 22nd September 1930. The Down slow line passed beneath the bridge arch on the right and ran behind the station fencing. There were no goods facilities at this station. A.Moss collection

The former platforms at Branston can just be discerned to the right of the Wolverhampton-bound service, in this diesel-era photograph. Author's collection

The Branston station site in June 1962, with platforms and railway cottages still intact. From here the track ran straight and level for another mile before starting a gradual rise towards Birmingham. B.W.L.Brooksbank.

Barton & Walton circa 1911. A section of fencing has been removed and a canopy erected in readiness for the arrival of the Royal Train. The Station Master, in traditional top hat attire for such occasions, observes the photographer, as does the police constable alongside the Phoenix Fire advertisement. Note the ladder between the rails. This station opened when the Birmingham & Derby Junction Rly commenced services on 12th August 1839, and it closed to passengers on 5th August 1958. However, the station buildings shown are not those built by the B&DJR. A Midland Railway Management Committee Minute of 20th September 1870, states that "Mr. Charles Humphrey's tender of £938 accepted for new station and buildings at Barton and Walton." The overbridge was also a later addition. An earlier Minute of 17th November 1857, records that the level crossing gates at Barton & Walton are to be repaired. It is believed the crossing was replaced by the road bridge around the time the new station was built. British Railways

The same buildings, but a much later period - early British Railways around 1952. The nameboard is standard LMS 'Hawkseye' style, introduced in the 1930's. Note the flowerbed, cultivated no doubt to beautify the station for entry to the 'Best Kept Stations' annual competition. All stations were encouraged to enter and prizes awarded. Author's collection

The road-side of the buildings with Station Master's residence included. These buildings were demolished in the early 1970's. V.R.Anderson

Barton and Walton station in June 1962, closed but still very much intact. The goods shed appears to be still in business as is the main line. Approaching the bridge, tender first on the Down line, is an Eastern Region O1 class 2-8-0 No.63789 running 'light engine'. B.W.L.Brooksbank.

War Department 2-8-0 No.90422 passes the 1907 signal box and the now severed track into the goods yard, with a southbound steel train from Scunthorpe for the West Midlands on 10th April 1965. This box closed four years later. Paul A.Forbes

No photographs are known to exist of the WYCHNOR JUNCTION station which the Midland Railway insisted was built for the interchange of passengers for services along the South Staffordshire Railway line to Lichfield. It opened on the 2nd April 1855, and closed on 1st August, 1856, when the Midland were forced to accede running rights over the line to Burton and Derby.

THE TUTBURY LINE - Opened to traffic September 1848

The North Staffordshire Railway had been formed in 1845 from a merger of several interests which had included a **Derby to Crewe Junction Railway**, and a branch they had proposed running from Tutbury into Burton. The new company continued with the proposal to construct the line via Tutbury to Derby, and the line from Tutbury into Burton. The Burton line was completed on 11th September 1848, ten months before completion of the North Staffs junction with the Midland Railway north of Willington station opened on 13th July 1849, to give a direct Potteries to Derby service.

With the opening of the Burton line, ten months before the direct Tutbury - Derby line opened, passengers travelling between the Potteries and Derby used the Tutbury - Burton services, and connections with Midland trains to and from Derby. However, it would appear that timetabled connections were not always kept, and there may have been irate passengers stranded at Burton, which the Midland were none too happy about.

A Minute from the Midland Management Committee meeting on 7th November 1848, ordered "that a pilot engine be sent to Burton station as soon as the sidings are made by the North Staffs company, for the purpose of working the goods train at that Junction, ... and also for bringing the passengers to Derby when they arrive too late from the North Staffs Railway, the latter company to pay for such special trains as are occasioned by their delay, at the rate of 2/- per mile one way". This Minute also records that this engine was also used for working the coal trade from the Swadlincote branch of the Midland.

For 35 years there were no intermediate stations. The line ran close to the villages of Rolleston-on-Dove, Stretton, and through Horninglow, and stations were later built for these locations. From Burton, the stations were as set out in the table below.

From Burton:	Opened	Closed
HORNINGLOW (1)	1/8/1883	1/1/1949
STRETTON & CLAY MILLS	1/8/1901	1/1/1949
ROLLESTON-ON-DOVE	1/11/1894	1/1/1949

Notes:
(1) Name later referred to in timetables as BURTON HORNINGLOW, BURTON-ON-TRENT (N.S.) HORNINGLOW and HORNINGLOW.

Timetabled passenger services were withdrawn from 1st January 1949, and the stations closed, although excursion trains called at Rolleston and Stretton for several years after this date. The attraction of a line to Burton was of course, access to the brewery and other traffic to and from the town. Whilst the North Staffs Railway had access to the town with the opening of this line, their sidings lay to the west of the main Midland Railway line and they relied on the Midland moving wagons between the breweries and the the North Staffs sidings. It was twenty years before the North Staffs Railway achieved direct rail access to the sidings complex on the east side of the Midland main-line, with the opening of a high-level line running from Stretton Junction, north of Horninglow station, and crossing both Derby Road and the main-line at Wetmore, and descending into sidings alongside those laid down by the L&NW Railway. The line opened initially as a single line from 1st April 1868, and it became double track from the 4th November 1873. This gave the North Staffs access to the Midland's Hay branch, which had been extended to link with the Midland's Guild Street branch at the Hay sidings, and then the brewery lines.

North Staffs and L&NWR access to these branches resulted from negotiations when the latter company was locked in a battle with the Midland, when each had made similar proposals for the construction of a new road bridge over the Hay meadows to carry the turnpike road out of the town towards South Derbyshire, and the demolition of the old bridge which in turn would allow rail access to the riverside area to be built.

Running powers were granted to the Great Northern Railway from July 1878, for the section of line between Dove Junction, a 100 or so yards section north of Rolleston-on-Dove station and through the high-level line into the Wetmore sidings, where the GNR laid its own sidings, goods sheds, engine turntable, water and coal facilities.

The line to Tutbury is perhaps most fondly remembered as the 'Tutbury Jenny' line, linking Burton with the former North Staffordshire main line at Tutbury. Here the $5^1/_2$ mile shuttle service provided a connection with trains between Derby, Uttoxeter, Stoke-on-Trent and onto Crewe. There were also connections with the Great Northern trains from Derby Friargate station to Uttoxeter and Stafford, which used running powers over the section of line between Egginton Junction and Uttoxeter for these services. At the Burton end of this service, connections were made with trains for Birmingham and Bristol, and stations to Leicester and Nuneaton, and the Lichfield, Walsall and Wolverhampton services.

On Saturdays there were three additional services from Burton, including one with the provision of through carriages to North Wales. The 10.30 am departure from Burton was an all-stations (except Marchington) service to Uttoxeter, where the carriages were attached to the 10.58 am ex Derby for Llandudno, arriving there at 3.5 pm. In the return direction, the 10.45 am departure from Llandudno conveyed through carriages for Burton, and these were added to the 'Jenny' service at Tutbury, arriving in Burton at 2.41pm. Patrick Webb's photograph on page 23 shows the through carriages from Llandudno attached to the Tutbury Jenny push-pull train.

The services via Tutbury to Crewe also gave access to west coast Scottish services, those to Liverpool and Manchester, Blackpool and the Fylde coast, and to North Wales, and they were heavily used in the years before express bus services and later the motor car era. Excursion traffic from the Leicestershire and South Derbyshire areas used this route as a gateway to the North Wales and North West coastal resorts.

Great Northern passenger services between Derby (Friargate) station and Burton also called at the stations to Rolleston-on-Dove. The GN services used the north-end bay

From the opening of the new station in 1883, North Staffs Railway services - the 'Tutbury Jenny' - used the bay platform at the north-end of the station, platform No.2. This view shows the 'Jenny' awaiting departure. The engine appears to be North Staffs No.11A, a class B 2-4-0T built at the company's Stoke works in 1874, and rebuilt with enlarged cylinders and a more enclosed cab in 1894 to give the engine crew greater protection in bad weather. The engine was withdrawn in 1916. Coaching stock is a mixture of four and six-wheel types, whilst on the adjoining track, stands a rake of L&NWR carriages. Authors collection

platform when the new Burton station opened on 29th April 1883. These trains were timetabled through to and from Grantham, via Ilkeston and Nottingham Victoria, with connections to London (King's Cross), and all parts of the GN system, which later became part of the London & North Eastern Railway.

The G N worked empty coaching stock from Derby (Friargate) to provide for the first train each morning, and back to Friargate after the last service into Burton, which suggests that the company did not wish to pay train stabling costs to the Midland.

The Tutbury line carried heavy train-loads of coal from the South Derbyshire and Leicestershire collieries to the Potteries, Manchester and the North-west, and there were return workings of empties, but also it was used by coal trains from the North Staffs area collieries to Leicester, Nuneaton and the metropolis. Fish and milk trains also ran daily, fish in the early mornings and often combined with parcels traffic, and milk in the early evenings. The LMS working timetable for September 1931, shows an LNER milk empties train leaving King's Cross at 6.10 am for Stafford Common, travelling via Grantham, Derby, Tutbury, Uttoxeter, arriving in Stafford around 2 pm.

The line was also used by through fitted freight trains between Camden (London) and Ancoats depot (Manchester), Camden - Carlisle, and Camden - Leeds, particularly during the early evening and overnight. These trains travelled from Nuneaton, to Overseal and the Leicester line into Burton, thence to the Burton - Tutbury line.

The former North Staffs line to Tutbury was closed in 1966 and the tracks lifted. The station buildings at Horninglow were used as a cafe through the early 1950's, and then boarded up, in which condition they remained through to the early 1980's.

(right) **The Derby road level crossing adjacent to the closed Horninglow station, taken from the 9.08 am to Tutbury in 1954. Beyond the signal box, weeds have taken over along the platform.** Patrick Webb

(opposite, middle) **5th July 1932, and the LMS 'Jenny', headed by former Midland 0-4-4T 1240 stands with two former North Staffs non-corridor carriages, No's 280 and 27, which were LMS 14883 and 14942 when this picture was taken. Beyond the fence, is the yard used by the LMS cartage fleet, with stables and vehicle storage area.** The late Dr. Jack Hollick

(right) **Horninglow station with its ornate brick panels within the timber framework. This view taken just after closure from the 1st January 1949, shows both the up and down side buildings and other timber sheds beyond the LMS 'Hawkseye' style nameboard. The crossing gate and cast-iron gate-post are North Staffs design, whilst to the right, there is a turnstile for pedestrians linked to the wooden barrow-crossing of the tracks.** G.L.Anthony

(left) **An early view of Stretton & Clay Mills soon after opening on 1st August 1901. This was the last station to be built on the Burton - Tutbury line, and not all the 'Tutbury Jenny' or GN trains called at this station. There was however, a provision that if passengers wished to alight from trains which were not timetabled to stop, they had to notify the guard on joining the train, and they were duly obliged. The platforms were built to take a long train, but they were later reduced in length by some fifty or so yards just before the overbridge.** V.R.Anderson collection

(opposite, top) **The North Staffs signal box close by Rolleston station on 20th September 1952. The brick base is of very similar type to that of the Stretton & Clay Mills ground frame shown on this page** F.W.Shuttleworth

A signal box structure does not appear to have been provided for this base, which is recorded as a ground-frame. This view was taken on 20th September 1952. The board which fronts the structure carries 'Stretton & Clay Mills' lettering. The frame was not installed when the station was first built, and the platforms may well have been shortened to allow its installation, since they originally extended up to the bridge from which this view was taken looking towards Burton. Sidings on the other side of the road bridge were controlled from this frame. F.W.Shuttleworth

An unidentified LMS 4F 0-6-0 passes Stretton & Clay Mills with an RCTS (Railway Correspondence & Travel Society) Railtour heading for Eggington Junction and the Derby Friargate line on 16th October 1965, some six months before the line was lifted. Note the track in the foreground which formed the Stretton goods siding. Paul A.Forbes

(right) **This LMS period view of Rolleston-on-Dove, looking towards Burton, shows how well-kept many of the branch line stations were in the pre-nationalisation era. Everywhere is tidy, the flower-beds are well tended, and whilst there are no passengers, or staff for that matter, to be seen, the view is a wholly pleasing one. The nameboard on the left is one of the LMS standard 'Hawkseye' types, which had small glass beads impregnated into the background to the lettering. These beads were intended to reflect the lights from carriages in darkness, and thus the name could be read.** D.Rokeby

Dove Junction signal box, on 25th August 1965, where the Great Northern line from Egginton Junction joined the North Staffs Tutbury line. A.Henshaw

Tutbury in North Staffordshire Railway days, with the 'Jenny' awaiting connections from Stoke-on-Trent. This view shows very clearly the pre-grouping scene: the NSR train, with a combination of four and six-wheel carriages, the station sign "Tutbury Change for Burton", water column, gas lamps, and even the two-wheel platform barrow, all make for a very evocative scene. Note too, the tidy trackwork, with fine ash rather than the chunky stone ballast of more modern times. V.R.Anderson collection

NSR DX class 0-6-2T No.77 built at Stoke in 1902, seen here approaching Tutbury and passing the Nestles factory. This engine, one of six in the class, was re-numbered 2239 by the LMS after Grouping in 1923, but was withdrawn in November 1927. The mixed freight train appears to be around 25 vehicles long and was typical of the workings along the North Staffs line through Tutbury prior to Grouping. The two Moira Colliery wagons are in the Nestles siding, no doubt unloading coal from the Leicestershire colliery. A.G.Ellis, courtesy A.Sommerfield

A Derby - Stoke service approaching Tutbury with No.8, a K class 4-4-2T built in 1911, heading three six-wheel carriages. The engine, re-numbered 2180 by the LMS in 1923, was one of seven 'K' class tanks built specifically for use on Crewe - Derby and Macclesfield - Stafford services. A.Sommerfield collection

The 'British Rail' Tutbury Jenny leaves for Burton, mid-afternoon on 23rd August 1952, with 58080, a former Midland 0-4-4T propelling the push-pull train. The fireman remained on the engine, whilst the driver controlled the train from a driving compartment in the end (leading) carriage. A.Sommerfield collection

LNER J3 0-6-0 No.4094 with a milk wagon and two carriages entering Tutbury with a Stafford - Derby Friargate train on 27th June 1933. The late H.C.Casserley

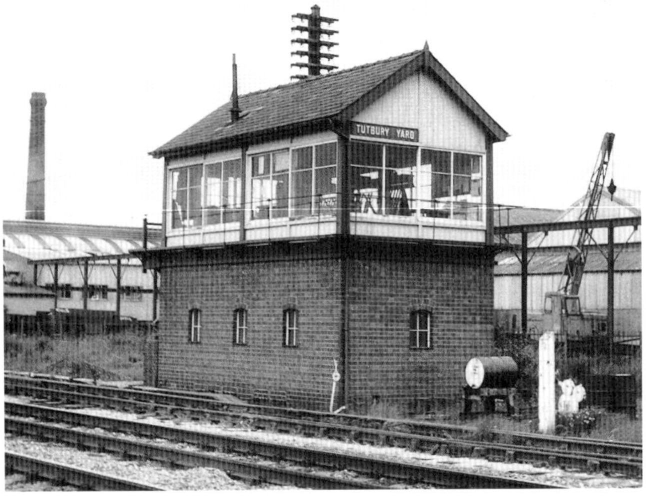

(above left) **Tutbury yard signal box to the west of the station on 24th June 1972. This was an LMS standard design box, not dissimilar to the L&NWR design, a late replacement for an earlier North Staffs structure.** A.Sommerfield

(above right) **Fronting the main A50 trunk road, and backing onto the railway goods and coal yard, was this 'slimline' office block, from which the local firm of Thomas Shipton Ltd., Coal, Coke and Lime merchants controlled incoming supplies by rail, and outward distribution by road.** Author's collection

J. C. Staton & Co. Ltd., were producers of gypsum rock in lump and ground form, and they had a private line from their works to the Tutbury Up station yard, worked by two saddle tank engines, one of which, No.2, a Manning Wardle engine built in 1883, is seen in the Tutbury yard in 1936. The late Dr. Jack Hollick

Staton's wagons were two-plank types, and four are seen in Staton's yard in June 1964. Livery was bauxite, with black-shaded white lettering. Gypsum rock is heavy, hence the need for only two-plank wagons. The engine shed is the black building in the background, whilst the archway gave rail access to the grinding mill. The late Dr. Jack Hollick

STRETTON JUNCTION TO WETMORE SIDINGS

(right) **The last signal box at Stretton Junction at the head of the North Staffs branch line giving access to the Wetmore sidings and Hay branch, originally authorised in 1863.View taken 31st January 1965.** R.Jeffcoat

(middle) **The branch from Stretton Junction crossed Derby Road at Wetmore, and here Class 5 4-6-0 44847 is heading a train of mineral empties from Colwick towards Wetmore sidings on 31st May 1966.** Paul A.Forbes

(below) **Class 8F 48279 heads up the incline out of Wetmore sidings to cross the Midland line and Derby Road, with a train of coal empties bound for Colwick yard, east of Nottingham, on 9th May 1966. Wetmore Road houses can be seen on the left of this picture.** Paul A.Forbes

THE LICHFIELD LINE - Opened to traffic 9th April 1849

From a junction with the Midland Railway at Wichnor, a line was planned through Lichfield to Walsall by the **Trent Valley, Midland & Grand Junction Railway Company**, formed on the 3rd August, 1846. At Walsall the line would link with the **South Staffordshire Junction Railway**, and provide a through route to Dudley and from there, a link with the Oxford, Worcester & Wolverhampton Railway.

The TVM&GJR, and SSJR, amalgamated their interests from the 9th July, 1847, to form the **South Staffordshire Railway Company**, and this company continued with the building of the line from Wichnor to Walsall. Within nine months of it opening, the Directors took the unusual step of leasing the line to the Company's former Chief Engineer and the Chief Clerk, on a 21 year lease from the 21st January 1850. They became responsible for all operations - perhaps this was a very early form of privatising railway operations!

The first few years were relatively uneventful, and the Company was allowed access through Wichnor Junction and over the Midland lines to Burton-on-Trent. However, this connection became the subject of some concern and when James Allport re-joined the Midland as General Manager in 1853, he decided to curb the running of South Staffordshire trains over the junction with the Midland. This gave rise to a new station and booking office facilities being built between the Midland and SSR lines, and passengers were required to change trains and re-book tickets. Sidings were also required to be laid for the exchange of wagons between the two companies, and merchandise was not required to be re-loaded. There was no road access to the Wichnor Junction area.

After eleven years of leased operation, the lease was transferred to the London & North Western Railway Company from 1st February 1861, and that company continued to operate the line until they finally absorbed the South Staffordshire Railway from 15th July 1867.

One of the more unusual railway incidents took place on 1st November 1861, when the L&NWR decided to challenge the Midland/Allport's continued refusal to reinstate through running at Wichnor Junction. The L&NWR train sent to run onto the Midland lines was met by a large number of Midland men, and an engine chained to the crossover. Access was stubbornly refused. The L&NWR train withdrew temporarily, but then returned some hours later, and with the Midland contingent gone, they were able to re-establish access. One month later full running powers were restored.

The line was increasingly used as the L&NWR gained traffic from and to the breweries in Burton. It gave the shortest access route from Burton to the company's own lines, both in the West Midlands via Lichfield, and Walsall, and through a connection at Lichfield Trent Valley, onto the North Western main line between London and the North-west, and via Carlisle to the Scottish railway company lines. Whilst the L&NWR had running powers over the North Staffs Railway line into Burton, that was a much longer route to reach it's own lines at Crewe.

L&NWR passenger services from Walsall and Lichfield ran through Burton to Derby, with timetabled connections via Lichfield Trent Valley to and from London, and the north. Connections were made at Burton with North Staffs trains, which in turn gave connections at Uttoxeter for Ashbourne, and thence by L&NWR train and all stations to the Spa town of Buxton. The first L&NWR train for Walsall shown in the 1908 timetable departed from Derby at 6.30 am calling at all stations, arriving at Walsall, forty miles distant, at 8.15 am. At Burton this train waited nineteen minutes before proceeding, with no apparent passenger connections, but most probably for off-loading milk, parcels and other items, and taking on merchandise for other stations on the line to Walsall and beyond. The first departure from Walsall was 7.15 am, arriving Derby at 8.55, with a delay at Lichfield T.V. of 21 minutes for connections with the London line. The 5.42 pm service from Derby connected at Burton with a Nottingham - Burton direct service. Connections at Lichfield City were made with Birmingham trains via Sutton Coldfield. Frequency of services on the Walsall - Derby line was generally nine trains each way right through to 1940, when it reduced to five each way during the war. After cessation of hostilities, trains from Walsall were terminated at Burton, with connections through to Derby and beyond. Prior to withdrawal of passenger services in 1965, trains were extended to and from Wolverhampton.

Four and six-wheel, and later bogie carriages, headed by 0-6-0 tender engines were the mainstay of services up to Grouping, and Midland and LMS 2P 4-4-0 tender engines, and later 2-6-4T engines gradually took over passenger services. In the mid-1950's British Railways introduced twin-car diesel multiple unit trains to replace steam-hauled services.

In addition to brewery related traffic using the line, coal from the South Derbyshire and Leicestershire coalfields was worked to Wichnor Junction, and short trains were re-assembled, before continuing out through the Lichfield line, into the West Midlands, and via the Trent Valley connecting line to the North-west main line for Stafford, Crewe and elsewhere, with trains of empties returning.

The Lichfield line from Wichnor remains open for freight traffic, and is also frequently used as a diversionary line for North-east - South-west passenger services, which sees High-speed HST 125 trains, and loco-hauled services passing through Alrewas, Lichfield Trent Valley and City stations, thence along the now-electrified line to Birmingham. When diversions are necessary, they have the effect of temporarily restoring passenger services between Burton and Lichfield City, primarily for passengers travelling to and from Tamworth.

The L&NWR signal box at the eastern end of Alrewas station, controlling the Croxall - Tamworth road level crossing. The crossing gates are standard L&NWR type, still in use on 5th February 1972. A.Sommerfield

No.2351, a former North Staffs 0-6-0 Class 159, built in 1900 by Nasyth Wilson & Co., shunting wagons in the goods yard at Alrewas on 20th May 1924. Here it is seen in LMS livery, and it continued in service until withdrawal in October 1936. W.L.Good

Lichfield Trent Valley Junction signal box in 1973 - note the abbreviated LMS name-board - controlled the approach to Trent Valley station, the level crossing, and the junction for the connecting line to the low-level West Coast main line. The road is now closed, but the signal box remains in use for the junction. Author

(opposite) **This view shows the fourth and final signal box, dating from 9th August 1953, at Wichnor Junction, alongside the Down main line. This was replaced by a ground frame from June 1969. The corrugated sheet lamp-hut on the right is of Midland Railway vintage.** M.A.King

(left) **Lichfield Trent Valley had High-level (Burton line) and Low-level (Euston-north) stations. This view shows the High-level looking towards Burton on 23rd March 1957, before a disasterous fire ravaged the High-level station buildings shortly afterwards.** The late H.C.Casserley

(middle) **Former Midland 4-4-0 2P, 395, a 17B Burton engine, working the 12.46 pm Derby - Walsall service, seen at Lichfield High-level on 25th September 1948, a 'high' day for the group on the right.** R.J.Buckley

(below) **This excellent view of the Low-level was taken on 10th October 1959, after fire had destroyed the High-level buildings. Looking south, the camera shows to good effect the former L&NWR signal box between the up and down fast lines, as well as the connecting line to the High-level (left). A 4F 0-6-0 and brakevan are on the high-level. The train from which the photograph was taken is typical of the long western-main-line semi-fast express trains, the odd one calling at Lichfield, notably the Windermere, Blackpool, or Liverpool services. In 1939 the northbound MANCUNIAN express was timetabled to stop at Lichfield Trent Valley at 6.21 pm, the third stop from leaving Euston. The morning, London-bound MANCUNIAN, ran non-stop Manchester - London.** The late H.C.Casserley

Low-level, on the 7th April 1939, and what better sight than streamlined Pacific, 6225 DUCHESS OF GLOUCESTER, resplendent in Crimson Lake and gold lining, at the head of a northbound express. E.R.Morten

(below) **An early-afternoon south-bound semi-fast express headed by re-built 'Royal Scot' 46119 LANCASHIRE FUSILIER. The high-level buildings and covered stairway were later destroyed by fire.** Author's collection

THE LEICESTER LINE - Opened from 1st August 1849

This was the last complete line to reach Burton, yet the eastern end from Leicester West Bridge to Bagworth, pre-dated the arrival of the first railway to reach Burton, the Birmingham & Derby Junction Railway. The 12 mile stretch of line out of Leicester was part of the **Leicester & Swannington Railway**, which opened for traffic to Bagworth from 17th July 1832, reaching Long Lane, later known as Coalville, in April 1833.

The Leicester & Swannington continued its independent operations until 1846, on the original route which was isolated from the developments which were taking place in the railway network in the late 1830's and early 1840's. Even though the Midland Counties Railway from Derby to Rugby passed through Leicester, the Leicester & Swannington's West Bridge terminus was a mile or so from the through line, and seperated by the River Soar.

When the **Midland Railway** was formed in May 1844 from an amalgamation of the Birmingham & Derby Junction, the North Midland and the Midlands Counties railways, it was the first sizeable merger of railway interests. And the Midland were soon looking to expand operations. In 1846 the L&S was taken over by the Midland and there were soon proposals tabled for extending the line from Coalville at the western end, through to Burton, and from Desford, to Knighton, to link with the Midland line south of Leicester. The line opened 1st August 1849, and the junction with the former Birmingham & Derby Junction line became known as Leicester Junction.

A junction for a branch to the village of Swadlincote was put in, some three miles from Burton, and this branch opened in 1851. A second branch line to Wooden Box, later named Woodville, was opened from 1st April 1859, and later still, in 1880, the two branches were linked to form a loop off the Leicester - Burton line. A colliery branch to serve the Stanton and Bretby colleries was built from the Swadlincote Junction sidings. The Leicester line was primarily a coalfields line, serving the south Derbyshire, central and north Leicestershire colleries, and the bulk of the traffic was coal, and coal empties. Stone from quarries at Bardon Hill and Glenfield accounted for considerable mineral traffic on the line. Heavy tonnages were moved out at both ends of the line, and via the Nuneaton line from Overseal which opened in 1872, and it is only since the closure of the colleries adjacent to the line in the late 1970's/early 1980's, that traffic has reduced to a trickle, with that being virtually all stone.

The line was strategically placed. Freight had two routes to London, out via Leicester Knighton Junction, or down the Nuneaton line from Overseal. The Burton end connection provided direct routes southwards to Birmingham and the Bristol line, via Lichfield to the North-west, via the Tutbury route to the Potteries and Manchester areas, and through Derby to the North Midlands and Yorkshire. The Leicester line was also a key route for Burton brewery traffic to the Bass warehouse housed beneath St. Pancras station London.

Through freight trains from the south destined for Manchester, and other northerly placed cities and towns, also used the route and the various through connections. Freight from Broad Street, Camden and Somers Town, all London freight terminals, passed over the Leicester - Burton line on its way to northern destinations.

Passenger services were primarily all-station 'stoppers' which provided connections at Leicester for London and the north, and at Burton for the South-west, Potteries and the North-west, and north via Derby. The average journey time was 70 minutes, but for a two-stations (Ashby & Coalville) stopping service, the journey time could be reduced to 52 minutes. At various times ,services were also provided between Coalville and Burton, Ashby and Burton, and Ashby and Leicester, with a few services scheduled over the Swadlincote - Woodville loop.

During the war years the line carried a number of troop trains, and munitions trains, being a secondary route away from the main trunk routes, and in the Second World War, less likely to attract the attention of enemy aircraft. Legend has it that during the war the driver of a train noticed what he thought could be an enemy aircraft above, and as he entered the Gresley tunnel, he stopped within the tunnel, allowing a little time for the aircraft to move away, before he proceeded.

Timetabled passenger services were withdrawn from the Swadlincote - Woodville loop from 6th October 1947, although the two stations remained open for excursion traffic until 8th September 1962. Passenger services between Leicester and Burton were withdrawn from 7th September 1964.

Excursion traffic ran regularly to a wide variety of destinations, not least Blackpool, Skegness, Scarborough, the North Wales resorts, as well as into the Derbyshire Peak District, and not forgetting Derby County and Leicester City football supporter specials.

Early passenger coaching stock was a variety of four and six-wheel types, followed by non-corridor bogie stock. From around 1950 corridor compartment stock found its way onto the branch services with increasing regularity. Motive power was provided by Leicester and Burton sheds, former Midland engines - 4-4-0 2P passenger, and 2F, 3F and 4F 0-6-0 tender freight engines dominated. The larger Class 5, 4-6-0 were regularly used, and there were occasional sightings of 'Patriot', 'Jubilee' and 'Royal Scot' types. Freight traffic was handled by the usual 0-6-0 types, the 2-6-0 'Crabs', the 8F 2-8-0's.

The line remains open, and there are plans to re-introduce peak hour passenger services, with a number of new stations to be built.

(opposite) **Leicester Junction (Burton) with the partly demolished engine shed in the background, and the junction signal box, on 10th June 1969. This signal box, dating from 1902, controlled the main line, the junction with the Leicester line, access to and from the engine sheds, and the connecting line to the Shobnall - Bond End branches.** M.A.King

Former Midland Railway 2P 4-4-0 No.40432, of 17B Burton shed, is waiting with a train of corridor stock for the Leicester service on 10th June, 1950. Leicester trains from Burton started either from the south-end No.3 bay platform, or from the main south-bound platform, No.4. The brewery building behind the train was the original Samuel Allsopp & Sons head office and new brewery. T.J.Edgington

Class 4F 0-6-0 44526 of Burton 17B, heads through Gresley towards Coalville with a train of coal empties in the early 1950's. The building immediately behind the engine may have been the original Gresley station building. Early plans show that the Burton to Nuneaton road crossed the line by level crossing, roughly where the engine is seen here. In 1866 the road bridge on which the photographer is standing was built and the level crossing was subsequently removed. By 1869 a new station had been built to the east of the road bridge. E.Woods

LMS 3F 0-6-0, 3247, trundles through Gresley station towards Leicester with a mixed freight in 1947. The single siding and crossover were removed and, around 1950, new extended wooden platforms were installed on the former siding area. E.Woods

The second Gresley station in the pre-1914 Midland period. The MR also owned the Burton & Ashby Light Railways, a street tramcar system which ran between Gresley station and Swadlincote, to join the main route between the Ashby-de-la-Zouch and Burton stations. One of the electric tramcars can be seen approaching the station (just above the ridge tiles on the 'Pearl' waiting

Swadlincote station in the early 1950's, when it was in use for regular excursion traffic and a parcels service. I can recall boxes of Palethorpes sausages from Tipton arriving by the early morning fish and parcels train, and being delivered by railway van to the Merchants grocery store in Belmont Street, Swadlincote in the early 1950's. The building under construction on the right is the then new Fire Station, and that, and the overbridge albeit, the road level has now been lowered, are the only links with Swadlincote's railway era remaining today (1997). This station was a mirror image of Woodville station. V.R.Anderson collection

(left) **2F 0-6-0 58258 shunts wagons from the daily goods and fish train which came from Burton arriving at approximately 7.30 am, and returned to Burton at around 8.20, often a brakevan and engine. The Swadlincote East signal box controlled the yard and trains in the section to Woodville. It was taken out of use on 23rd January 1955, and the structure removed to Shobnall sidings as a replacement at that location. A pedestrian footbridge once stood next to the wooden barrow crossing in the foreground.** E.Woods

(below) **Swadlincote goods yard, just before removal of tracks, after an overnight dusting of snow. The line to Woodville is on the left, with the track into the timber goods shed (out of picture) on the right.** The late C.D.Campton

THE GREAT NORTHERN RAILWAY CONNECTION - Opened 1st July 1878

A combination of new line from Derby Friargate station to Rolleston-on-Dove on the North Staffordshire Railway line, and running powers from there, brought the Great Northern Railway to Burton. The eastern counties of England were good grain growing areas and much of it was brought to Burton, to satisfy the requirement for the huge quantities of barley required by the malsters and brewers. The GN connection thus opened up a direct through route for this traffic.

Running powers from Dove Junction, Rolleston included use of the North Staffs Horninglow branch line from Stretton Junction, across the Midland main-line, and into Wetmore sidings. The GN proceeded to develop their own goods sidings and warehouses, and engine servicing facilities between the L&NW and NSR sidings and Wetmore road, and a connection with the Midland's Hay branch at the Salt's Maltings junction. The GN was also granted running powers over the Midland main line from the North Stafford junction at Horninglow, into Burton station. From the opening of the new Burton station in 1883, the GN shared use of the No.2 bay platform with the North Staffs services.

GN passenger services called at the intermediate stations on the line out to Rolleston-on-Dove, giving these relatively small villages a total of between eighteen (weekdays) and twenty-three (Saturday) Burton services each way, inclusive of the Tutbury services - a very good service for a secondary line. Coal and mineral traffic, and the inevitable brewery traffic used the GN route to the eastern counties right up to final closure.

The route from Burton to Derby Friargate, via Dove Junction, was 1 1/2 miles longer than the direct Midland route. Journey times were substantially longer, average 32/33 minutes, against the 17 minutes for non-stop Midland trains. The GN's Friargate station was however, considerably closer than the Midland station to the Derby town centre. The GN and later London and North Eastern Railway services operated through Ilkeston and Nottingham to Grantham and gave connections to and from the London (King's Cross) - East Coast main line. Regular excursions to the East Coast resorts of Skegness and Mablethorpe used the GN route.

Had the original 1865 proposals for a **Burton-on-Trent & Nottingham Railway** come to be built, it would have provided a more direct route to Nottingham. The proposals were for the line to commence at Hawkins Lane, run out via Repton, Twyford, Castle Donington and onto Nottingham. Alas, it was not to be.

(below) **The Great Northern goods warehouse and sidings at Wetmore, with the loco water tower in the distance, shown out of use on 31st April 1966. The provision of five storage sidings in addition to the track serving the loading bay, gives a good indication that GN traffic volumes to the town must have be considerable. In later years 8F 2-8-0s were known to have been used shunting the former GN/LNER sidings.** R.Jeffcoat

(left) **The rather sparse locomotive servicing facilities consisting of a turntable, coaling stage, water crane and tank were installed by the GN at Wetmore yard. Only a handful of engines used the facilities each day, and towards the end of the steam era, engines visited the former Midland shed for coaling and other servicing.** R.Jeffcoat

(above) **The GN turntable, capable of turning a V2 2-6-2 tender engine but not often called upon to do so.** R.Jeffcoat

(left) **Behind the GN yard, and alongside Wetmore Road nearer to Anderstaff Lane, a further large grain warehouse was built, seen here on the opposite side of the sleeper fence which fronted Wetmore Road.** Author

MIDLAND RAILWAY BRANCHES WITHIN THE TOWN

Beer casks and incoming supplies of grain, hops and coal by rail led to a considerable growth in the number of horse-drawn vehicles required to transport supplies between the railway yard and the various breweries. As a result the town streets became ever more congested.

In 1859 the Midland Railway succeeded in obtaining 'The Midland Railway and Burton upon Trent Bridge Act' which authorised the construction of the first branch railway from the main line towards the Hay area of the town, where the largest brewery, Bass & Co, was located. The inclusion of 'Bridge' was a necessity, as the road bridge across the Hay meadows and the river would require replacement by a new bridge which would give sufficient height for railway traffic to pass beneath. The Midland fought the London & North Western Railway company for the right to build branches to the Hay meadows, and construct the new bridge. The L&NWR were the first to secure the Marquis of Anglesey's support as landowner, for their proposed Bill, but the Midland objected strongly. Eventual agreement led to the L&NW and Midland proposed Bills to be amalgamated, and this resulted in the 1859 Act being enacted. Land from the Marquis was made available in return for the railway companies agreement to be responsible for all costs and maintenance of the new bridge, and to admit the North Staffordshire Railway to the scheme if required.

The Hay Branch was the first of seven branches to be commenced as main arterial routes through the town, and a large number of private sidings were connected to these. The Midland was responsible for track and signal maintenance on each of the branches, and also for a distance of between one and four-chains-length on each of the private sidings directly connected to the branch. A 'Limit of track maintenance' board indicated where the private siding commenced. The brewery companies paid the Railway company for maintenance of the private siding connections, but other maintenance costs were borne by the railway company, and they sought to cover their costs through charging for wagon usage and transportation of loads. The table below gives the dates when each of the seven Midland branch lines opened.

These threaded right through the centre of the town, and few streets were without a railway level crossing right up to the 1960's. To most people the lines they saw crossing the streets were the brewery lines, but this was not so, despite the fact that all trains were headed by one of the brewery company engines. An 1845 Act of Parliament required that all road crossings of railway lines had to be gated and attended by railway staff for safety reasons, but it was not until 1861/2 that the first branch crossed one of the streets - that was at Anderstaff Lane. This was not the first level crossing in Burton, there were those on the main line at Moor Street, Cat Street Lane (later Station Street), adjacent to Burton station, and at Old Wetmore, when the Birmingham & Derby Junction Railway first opened. Midland Railway crossing gates, signal boxes and equipment were used where the Midland branches crossed the streets, but many of the crossings on private siding lines were provided with outside contractors equipment and signal boxes. Standard MR signals and signalling equipment was used, except where the L&NW track, from their sidings, crossed the Hay branch at Hawkins Lane and into that company's goods yard.

THE HAY BRANCH	- **North Staffs Jct to the Hay**	
	Opened to Anderstaff Lane	November 1861
	Anderstaff Lane to the old Burton Trent bridge	30th November 1862
	Line completed along the Hay	6th November 1864
	- **Sanders Branch** off the Hay Branch at Hawkins Lane Jct	
	To Worthington's Maltings and Allsopp's Cooperage	November 1861
	Burton Brewey off Sanders Branch	November 1861
GUILD ST. BRANCH	- **Guild St. Branch Junction to the Hay**	
	Horninglow Bridge across Guild St. and High St. to the Hay	4th October 1862
MOSLEY ST. BRANCH	- **Mosley St. Branch Junction (Burton station south) to Ind Coope's Station Street**	13th March 1865
HORNINGLOW BRANCH	**Horninglow Branch Junction to Horninglow wharf**	27th February 1873
SHOBNALL BRANCH	- **Wellington St. Junction to Shobnall wharf**	28th April 1873
BOND END BRANCH	- **Wellington St. Junction to Bond End wharf**	2nd December 1875
	Sidings from Dale St. Junction to Trent Brewery	
	Sidings from Uxbridge St. Junction to Walkers Brewery and Riley's timber yard.	
	To Charrington's Maltings, and to Peach's Maltings	
	From James St. Junction, the Park St. branch, to Robinson's Brewery, and the Duke St. Branch.	
DALE ST. BRANCH	- **Dale St. Junction** (Bond End Branch) **to Leicester Junction - Sidings Junction**	25th February 1884

THE HAY BRANCH

(above) **Two photographs which give a wonderful panoramic view of the Hay branch (left), the Sanders branch with the line of wagons awaiting collection, the L&NW coaling stage and re-roofed engine shed. The 4F 0-6-0 44248 is pulling out of the L&NW sidings with an evening beer train bound for Mold Junction near Chester in June 1954. This was the view from the old Hawkins Lane bridge.** Patrick Webb

Movement of wagons in the early days was by shunting horse, but attention soon turned to steam locomotives and a local builder, Thornewill & Wareham. Bass Ratcliffe & Gretton took delivery of their first steam engine in 1861 and this was followed two years later by a second locomotive. In the years thereafter, steam engines were purchased by a number of the brewery companies, and all were given quite distinctive and colourful liveries.

In the early 1930's private locomotives running over railway company owned lines such as the town branches, were required to be 'plated' to indicate they had been passed fit for working these lines.

The 1960's saw the demise of the brewery sidings and the town branches. The costs of maintaining the lines was high and it is reputed that the British Railways Chairman, Dr. Beeching, when advised of the financial arrangements and the heavy maintenance costs, decreed that the brewery company users should cover all costs. This led to the breweries making arrangements to move loads by road, and within the brewery premises, by pipeline, and within a relatively short period the town's rail web was being removed.

(below) **Hawkins Lane junction signal box on the Hay branch dated from 1929. This signal box controlled the junction with the Sanders branch, the L&NW lines and access from the North Staffs Wetmore sidings also. The diesel shunter is moving from the L&NW yard.** J.Miller

(right) **The Anderstaff Lane level crossing along Wetmore Road.** Author's collection

The new Trent Bridge was opened on 22nd June 1864 with construction costing more than £22,000. It was 469 yards long and 30 feet wide including walkways. By the early 1920's it required widening to cope with the increasing road traffic, as well as the tramcars of the Burton Corporation and Burton & Ashby Light Railways. Between 1924 and 1926 the north-side of the bridge was moved outwards by 20 feet to give an overall inside width of 50 feet. In this view, widening at the town end (Bridge Street) is underway. One of Worthington's brewery engines is seen on the Hay branch, immediately below the Burton Corporation tramcar heading off the bridge (Burton & Ashby tramcars were all open toppers - the one shown has a roof). Note the extended length of the tram wire brackets (right of centre), and the shorter bracket of the pole (left of centre), yet to be re-located when that section of the bridge is completed. Author's collection

(right) **As the Hay branch turned alongside the river, a private siding into the Burton Gas Works, which also extended to the Electricity works,was controlled by the Salt's Engine Shed signal box. This view shows the coke handling plant in the gas works yard, and the close proximity of the siding to the riverside.** Author's collection

(middle and bottom) **Two views of the Hay wharf alongside the swollen River Trent in December, 1910. The new Trent Bridge, from which this view was taken, was higher than the old wooden road bridge it replaced so that rail traffic could pass along the Hay branch. As the railway approached the bridge, the gradient dropped and whenever the river flooded its banks, Hay sidings were inevitably submerged. Traffic movements were reduced, but flooding did not normally close the line.** J.S.Simnett (both)

A morning scene in the Hay sidings in 1953, with two of the Bass engines at work. The one on the right is coming off the Guild Street branch. Patrick Webb

Worthington No.1, on the Hay branch in April 1956, whilst a Bass engine can be seen behind the two rear wagons. The whole of the area shown has been re-developed since closure of the branch lines through the town, and only the water tower, seen on the extreme left, and more clearly in the previous picture, still remains as a landmark today. Patrick Webb

Guild St. branch left the main line at Guild St. Branch Junction, seen here curving off to the left behind the Horninglow Bridge signal box, and the former Midland No.1 Grain warehouse. The view was taken on 12th April 1969. M.A.King

A few hundred yards from the junction the branch straightened before it crossed the siding which went from the L&NWR yard alongside Hawkins Lane into Allsopp's brewery. The crossing is seen here on 10th September 1967, out of use, with the adjacent Midland signal box in course of removal. R.Jeffcoat

The 1889 signal box at the main Guild St. level crossing, 27th July 1964. The box is complete with the original Midland Railway round-end name board in the early fixing position. Note the cast sign hanging from the front of the box proclaiming: "Caution - when the bell rings these gates will be opened" - a standard fixture on all street crossing boxes. Note too the standard claxon bell, which caused many an aspiring Olympic athelete to sprint to beat the closure of the gates, and avoid missing the bus! The poster advertises cheap trips to Manchester, Liverpool and New Brighton. M.A.King

The area bounded by High Street, Station Street and Guild Street, contained a number of brewery owned lines and wagon yards, and Bass No.3 is seen here during shunting operations on 17th September 1958. M.E.J.Dart

An unusual building stood for many years behind the buildings fronting High Street. Seen on 10th June 1969, it was constructed from standard MR signal box sections, including a roof complete with Midland wooden finials. Two theories have been voiced - (1) that the sections came from a dismantled box - (2) that when the Midland were erecting signal boxes along the town branches, they brought sections in bulk, and those left over were used to construct this office.

The larger of the two level crossings on High Street is open for the passage of modern motive power, Bass No.7, an 0-4-0 30 ton diesel locomotive built in the Burton workshops of E.E.Baguley Ltd. Burton Daily Mail

The second High Street level crossing, a single-track brewery owned crossing, was next to the Blue Posts Inn, and here Worthington No.6, an 0-4-0 saddletank, crosses on its way to the Worthington Line Junction, at the end of the Hay branch sidings. M.E.J.Dart

The Blue Posts crossing and signal box on 3rd June 1963. Certain features suggest this box may have been constructed using very early MR signal box panels, particularly as the crossing gates are the original standard Midland pattern with vertical bars, and the signal is a standard Midland post and arm with spot rather than the later straight sided black stripe. J.Miller

The view from the Blue Posts level crossing towards the Hay. The junction and line to the right was a short siding behind the end of the Hay branch. This mid-1950's view shows the Midland lower quadrant signal with the early black spot marking. D.L.F.Gilbert

MOSLEY ST. BRANCH

(above) **Mosley St. branch commenced alongside the south end of the station and was a relatively short one, just over one quarter mile long. This early view, of circa 1880, shows the private siding to the Bass waterworks on the left, whilst the main track runs on towards Mosley St. and Station Street where it served Ind Coope's yard and spirit stores. Note the inside-keyed track (left of wagon) and primitive point-work. This area included the Ind Coope new cooperage, hence the stack of barrels on the right.** Author's collection

(right) **The Mosley St. level crossing at the entrance to Ind Coope's 'new' cooperage yard on 7th August 1965.** R.Jeffcoat

SHOBNALL BRANCH

The Shobnall branch commenced from a junction with the main Birmingham - Derby line and swept through ninety degrees past the Sharp, Bros & Knight timber yard and across Wellington Street. This view shows the curved section, with the private siding which served both the Baguley Car Company and Sharps timber yard. Very few passenger trains traversed this route, and this one is the RCTS THE MERCIAN, which had used the Dallow Lane branch from Stretton junction to Shobnall junction, and is seen approaching the main line junction which was controlled by the Leicester Junction (Burton) signal box. Date - 2nd June 1957. Engine - Black 5 No.45091. T.J.Edgington

(left) **These are the old Midland signals which controlled access from the Shobnall branch to the main line. The short-arm signal was for movements along to the engine shed at Leicester junction, the other for crossing to the down main running lines. Date - 27th July 1964.** M.A.King

(below) **This view from the iron footbridge which crossed the Shobnall branch and adjacent Bass sidings, shows the Shobnall branch from the Wellington Street signal box, and entrance to the Bass sidings on the right where a latter day Sentinel shunter goes about its business.** D.L.F.Gilbert

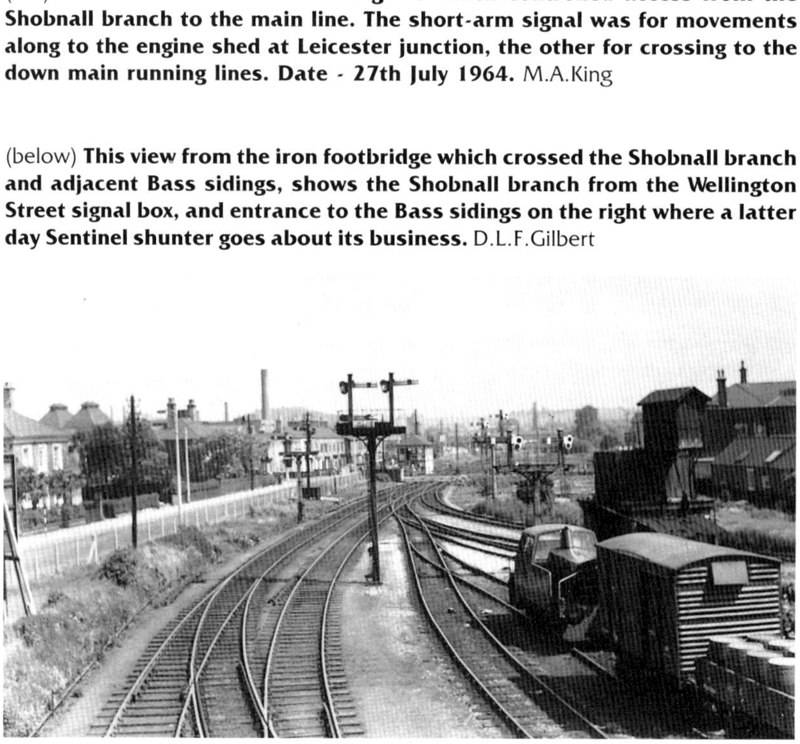

(right) **Wellington Street Junction signal box which controlled the adjacent level crossing, the main line connection and from where the Bond End branch commenced.** M.A.King

(middle) **One of the Midland 0-4-0T engines built for use on the tightly curved sections of the Burton branches. No.1535 heads a mixed freight off the L&NW Dallow Lane branch through Shobnall junction on 27th June 1933. The signal box, a replacement installed in December 1917, controlled the first seven chains of the Dallow branch, the line to the Trent & Mersey Canal Shobnall wharf, and entrance to the Marston Thompson & Eversheds Albion brewery private siding. Note the very tidy trackwork.** The late H.C.Casserley

(below) **Twenty years after the previous view, the Shobnall sidings complex alongside the Shobnall junction signal box. The Dallow Lane branch is seen curving away to cross under Shobnall Road, whilst Marston's brewery's chimney and buildings are in the background. Former Midland 0-4-0T 41536, an unidentified 0-6-0T, and one of the Baguley 0-4-0 diesels bring life to this area.** Patrick Webb

(above) **The end of the Railway company maintenance was a few yards beyond this bridge over the canal, from where the Marston's siding commenced.** R.Jeffcoat

(left) **One of the early Midland cross-bar signals in use at Shobnall sidings. This type was used where lines crossed, or where two lines came together round sharp curves, and were considered more effective than individual signals for each line: two lines were effectively controlled by one signal. The bar face-on, as shown, was the signal for an approaching train to stop, and when turned end-on, the right-of-way was given.** M.A.King

(below) **Worthington's brewery were a large user of the small Planet 0-4-0 engines, and No.21 is seen here shunting wagons in the Shobnall yard. They were originally petrol driven and later converted to diesel.** R.Newman

Baguley diesel No.6 shunts the Shobnall yard with two of the internal user specially built vans for the Bass Grain Dept. M.E.J.Dart

Allsopp's Shobnall maltings, alongside Shobnall Road, were served by a private siding off the Dallow Lane branch, and here ex-LMS 3F 0-6-0T No.47464 picks up bulk grain wagons for Shobnall yard during the latter days of steam working. R.Jeffcoat

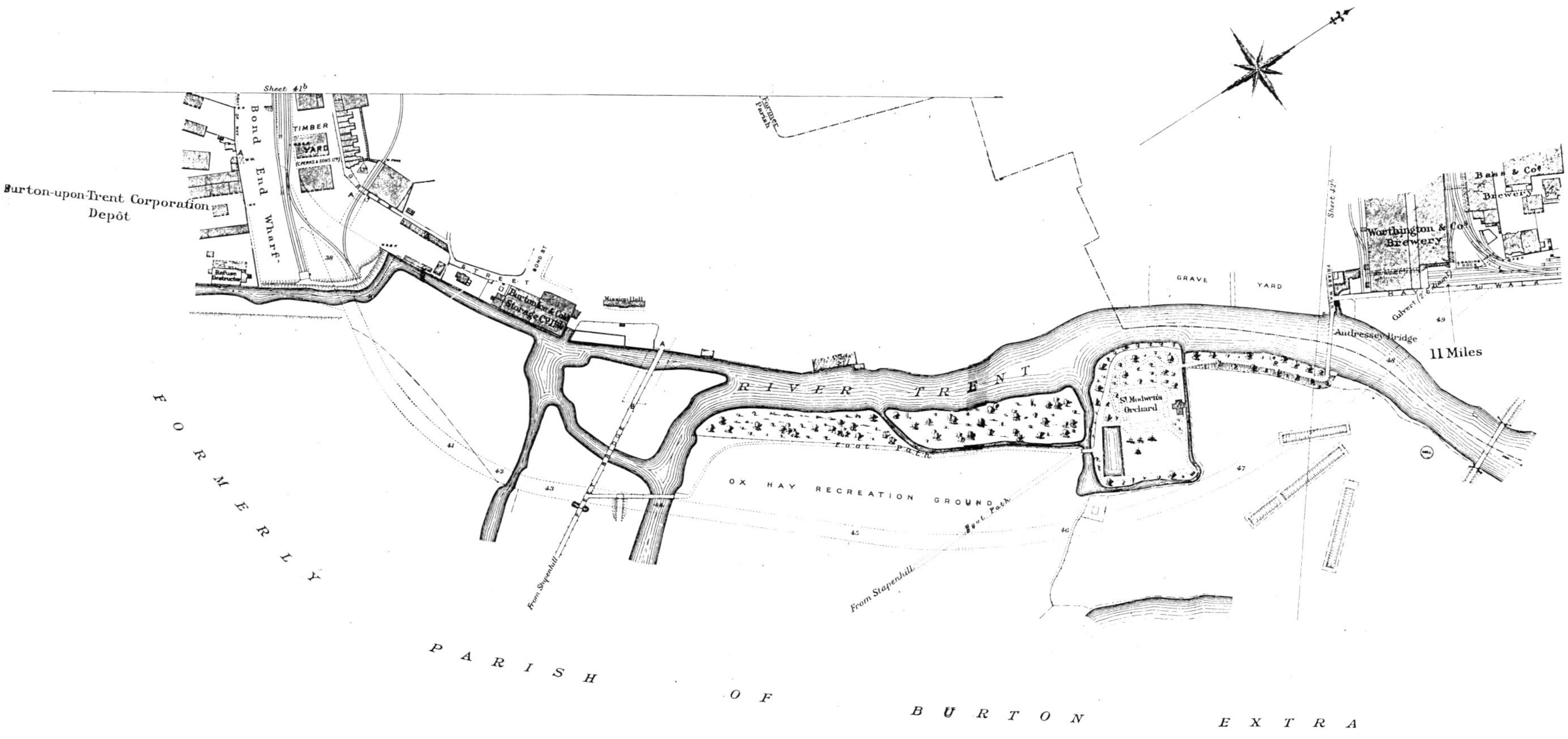

A survey, dated August 1923, which shows the route proposed in 1868 for a Midland line between the Bond End Branch and the Hay Branch which was never built. The LNWR also had a scheme to link the two branches but that also never came to fruitition.

Bond End branch commenced from Wellington Street junction with the Shobnall branch, and virtually the whole of this branch was on land reclaimed when the Burton Canal was filled in during 1872. Open cab 0-6-0T 41839 is seen heading towards Bond End and is about to pass beneath the main Birmingham - Derby line. The land on the right was where the first siding to the canal wharf was built when the railway arrived in the town in 1839. Moor Street is behind the fence. Cattle wagons taken out of livestock service were used increasingly for beer barrel traffic in the 1950's, and the third vehicle is one such wagon. The late H.C.Casserley

The branch dipped beneath the main line, seen here with 0-4-0ST 41523 travelling 'light engine' towards Wellington St. junction, and 4F 0-6-0 44580 heading a parcels train on the main line, 2nd June 1950. Burton canal originally occupied the ground that the Bond End tracks are on, and the overbridge was put in to replace a drawbridge following a disaster on Saturday morning 31st October 1846, when the driver of a train, approaching the drawbridge in dense fog, failed to see that it was open for canal traffic, and closed for trains. The engine tipped into the canal and closed the railway line and canal for several days thereafter. Note the MR signal has lost its finial. The late H.C.Casserley

The Dale Street signal box which controlled the level crossing and access to the Dale Street Branch which ran through Worthington and Peach's Maltings sidings to Leicester Junction Sidings Junction signal box. Access to the L&NWR coal yard was also controlled from this signal box, seen here 27th July 1964. M.A.King

(above) **The impending closure of the Burton branches and brewery sidings generated much interest amongst railway enthusiasts and a number of railtours descended on the town. This LCGB (Locomotive Club of Great Britain) special is seen at Bond End, with eager eyes savouring the 'last' journey, and one of the very few passenger workings over the Burton branches. Ivatt 2P 2-6-2T 41328, fitted for push-pull working is at the head of the train.** Patrick Webb

(left) **Branston Road signal box and entrance to Bond End wharf from Branston Road 27th June 1965, virtually at the point of closure.** R.Jeffcoat

There were several additional Midland owned small branches off the Bond End branch with access to them controlled by the Uxbridge St. junction and the James St. junction signal boxes. James St. junction signal box was sited between two 'main' lines, one seen to the left which crossed Park St., New St., and Duke St., and the track to the right which also crossed Park St. New St., from where a private siding crossed Station St., to provide access to Worthington's new brewery complex, and then crossed High Street at the Blue Posts crossing to give access to the Hay sidings - a through route indeed! Note the bi-directional signal. The building behind was Eadie's cooperage, and prior to that had been the Thornewill & Wareham locomotive works. 3rd July 1966. R.Jeffcoat

Eadie's cooperage is seen in this view as the track from James St. junction crosses Park St No.1 level crossing on the Duke St. branch. The signal is located by the Up line to aid visibility for trains coming round the tight bend from James St. R.Jeffcoat

The Park St. No.1 signal box on 27th July 1964. Installed in 1902, the box was erected with a lower than normal height base. M.A.King

From Duke St. the Bass private siding went onto cross Station Street. A Royal visit to Bass brewery took place on the 29th June 1929, when H.R.H. The Prince of Wales, seen walking towards the Station St. crossing, initiated a special brew, which when bottled as 'Princes Ale', became a sought after drink, and has since become a collectors item if you're lucky enough to find an un-opened bottle! Author's collection

The end of the branch at Duke St., where there were in fact two sets of level crossing gates side by side, the one set serving Bass sidings behind the photographer. The other line served Eadie's brewery. New Street No.1 crossing and signal box are seen in the distance. M.A.King

Neglect and decay. The second line from James Street crossed both Park Street No.2 and New Street No.2 crossings. 0-4-0ST No.47000 crosses New Street No.2 crossing just prior to the closure of this branch in 1968. The Persil obviously has not been used on either the signal box or the locomotive. R.Newman

From New Street No.2 level crossing, the branch continued towards Station Street splitting, with one line to Robinson's brewery, the other crossing Station Street by means of a small private level crossing alongside the former Mayor's Arms public house, seen here on 22nd October 1967. R.Jeffcoat

The Robinson's brewery private siding was only a short stretch of line, which curved tightly round to a loading dock to terminate behind Tarver's Ladies and Gents Outfitters shop in Station Street (right), seen here on 8th August 1965. This was probably the least photographed siding ever! R.Jeffcoat

This view of Worthington's shows a wealth of detail, not least what appears to be two wagon loads of 'spent' hops (hops after mashing) in the foreground. This appears to be the cooperage yard - the barrel makers. The GN wagons in this and other views serve to emphasise the amount of traffic to and from the eastern counties. J.S.Simnett

Between the buildings, a typical Bass roadway paved with stone-setts. Even after the arrival of steam engines the breweries continued to use horses to move wagons around the yards, and here one is seen pulling a loaded wagon towards the photographer. This view is taken looking towards the smaller of the two Guild St. level crossings. J.S.Simnett

(below) **After removal of many of the warehouses in the yards just north of the station, Ind Coope retained rail access and their private sidings were laid into concrete as seen to the left of this picture. The British Rail track was slewed to link with the new siding configuration. Diesel class 08, No. 08014, is seen on 28th June 1978, delivering a consignment of bulk grain to the brewery, from where Ind Coope's own locomotive would move the wagons. This was the newest, and last of the brewery private sidings.** A.O.Wynn

ENGINE SHEDS

The earliest locomotive servicing facilities in Burton were those provided in 1847, when a Midland Railway Minute dated 29th June, records ..."that a supply of water for engines be forthwith made at the Burton station". This was followed on 15th August 1848, by a further Minute,...."ordered a larger water tank be erected at Burton station".

On the 12th March 1849, it was reported that tenders had been received for the erection of an Engine Shed at Burton, and Thomas Green's tender for £362 was accepted. A further, larger, water tank at Burton station was required by Mr. Kirtley for engines and this was approved on 10th July 1849. The first coke stage and line, and an engine pit, were approved on the 25th September 1849. A further Minute of 16th January, 1850, records..."Engineer to erect coke stage and build two engine pits at the Burton station, and also alter the sidings on the engine lines as required by the Locomotive Committee". There is a reference in a Minute on 1st June 1852, to..."Turntables extended to 37' 6" at Burton". Further alterations to the engine shed and coke stage were authorised at a meeting on 1st July 1856.

In 1856 a fatal accident was reported to have resulted from the engine turntable and a siding being too close, and on the 16th December that year, an order was made..."for the siding near the engine turntable to be slewed so as to prevent engines being turned coming into collision with other engines or carriages standing on the siding".

The Locomotive Department made application on 1st November 1859 for additional engine sidings to be installed at Burton Junction - most probably the location where the Leicester line came in, south of the station. There appears to be no other mention of Burton Junction in the Midland Minutes, but the North Staffordshire Railway Company referred to its junction with the Midland at Horninglow, as 'Burton Junction'. The Midland used the name 'North Stafford Junction'.

An indication that 'Sheer legs', - a large tripod arrangement of substantial timbers used with block and tackle equipment - had been installed prior to 1863 for the lifting of engines and tenders, comes from a Minute of 6th October that year, when it was ordered ".....they be lengthened". At the same meeting an order was made for the sand furnace to be rebuilt and a roof erected between the tank house and the shed. Foundations for a new engine turntable were approved in January 1864, and in May 1865 essential repairs to the engine shed roof were necessary. Further work to drain the engine pits at the station was carried in early 1866 by a Mr E.Dus-Antoy.

The engine shed and servicing facilities adjacent to the station continued in use until the opening of a new engine shed alongside Leicester Junction on 29th April 1870. Land was purchased in February 1869 from the Marquis of Anglesey and the first 'round house' building and trackwork constructed at a total cost of £16,100. Traffic to and from Burton had been increasing continuously since the arrival of the B&DJR, and the opening of the new engine shed kept pace with the increased engine servicing requirements. The growth of the railway network and increasing traffic to and from Burton, gave rise to longer-distance train workings by Midland enginemen, not only those based at Burton, but from other Midland engine sheds also. Traffic workings were round-the-clock, and enginemen working into Burton often required sleeping accommodation before making an outward working back to their home depot. The Midland therefore sought tenders for the erection of 'Engine Drivers Lodgings', and at a meeting on 14th May 1872, Edward Bennett's tender of £1,186.1s.4d, was accepted.

Construction of a new Coaling Stage was authorised on 20th April 1875 and this was built soon afterwards. By the 18th January 1876, the Locomotive Department were seeking Management Committee authority to have the coal stage 'boarded-up' on one side. The Management's response was an enquiry as to whether "this is the only stage which requires enclosing amongst the many others ordered during the previous two years?". Authority for boarding-up was given one month later on 29th February 1876, and it is therefore probable that this was the first coaling stage to be boarded

An early morning view of Burton, ex-MR, shed yard on 28th July 1946, with a number of 0-6-0 and 4-4-0 engines ready for duty. L&GRP

The roundhouse shed behind the Leicester Junction (Burton) signal box on 3rd May, 1969 after the shed section next to the running lines had been demolished. The enginemen's lodging house built around 1873, is seen on the extreme right. M.A.King

on one side, with others including the one at Kettering being boarded later. Enginemens' Mess Room and shed office facilities were approved in November 1875.

At the Management meeting on 2nd January 1877, a requirement for a coal stage and water tank sidings at Wetmore and the Dixie sidings was discussed, and plans were ordered to be made. This is a further indication of the increasing traffic requirements and the need to reduce the time lost each time an engine had to travel from the Dixie sidings to the engine shed for coal and water, and would allow more intensive use of engines, but it is believed it never got beyond the plan-stage. However, a second 'Round House' for 24 engines was built on land between the existing round house and the main line, and this opened in 1892 at a cost of £12,260. One of the last alterations made by the Midland company was the conversion of the earth toilets to water closets in 1912.

The diameter of the turntables installed in the two round-house engine sheds were adequate for turning Midland engines, and could also turn any visiting engines from the other companies running into Burton. However, the merging of the Midland with other companies to form the London Midland & Scottish Railway from the 1st January 1923, brought the possibility of larger engines from some of the other companies, notably the L&NWR, being used on turns to Burton. The LMS therefore provided larger turntables, a 57' replacement for the 42' diameter table in No.1 shed, and a 55' replacement for the 50' table in No.2 shed.

When the Midland numbered their engine sheds, Burton became No.2, Derby being the No.1. It retained No.2 as part of the Midland Division created at the 1923 Grouping, and in the 1935 re-numbering scheme, the shed became 17B to the area shed, 17A Derby. Further re-organisation in 1963 led to the shed becoming 16F as a sub-depot of Nottingham. The engine sheds remained in use through to the end of steam in 1968.

Other Company engine shed facilities included a small four-road shed and turntable for North Staffs engines at the north-end of the station, located alongside the Midland's

This Midland Railway locomotive was originally built as a 6' 6" Single by E.B.Wilson & Co in 1848, and rebuilt as an 0-6-0 well tank in November 1875. It survived into LMS ownership in 1923 renumbered as 1605 but was withdrawn the following year. It is seen here, circa 1920, on the short stretch of track at the rear of the 1870 roundhouse, with the watertank building to the left. J.A.Sommerfield collection

(left) **An evocative shot of 0-6-0T 47313 facing the daylight on 15th November 1964. This photograph encapsulates much of the steam shed scene and atmosphere of yesteryear - the whitewashed walls, the odd few engine springs lying around, the notice-board found at the entrance to every engine shed, the blackened brick-work reflecting more than ninety years of non-stop use, and not least the dark shed interior.** Paul A.Forbes

(below) **Interior of the Horninglow shed on 13th July 1947, soon after re-roofing, with 1932 Kitson built 0-4-0ST 7000 alongside a Fowler 3F 0-6-0T No.7641.** The late H.C.Casserley

Derby Street coal yard. This opened in 1865 and remained in use until damaged by fire in 1925, when the shed was demolished. The tracks and a small turntable remained in situ until the 1970's, and it is probable that the turntable was the one authorised by the Midland in January 1864. Prior to the opening of the NSR shed, their engines used the Midland facilities by the station, but increasing congestion led to their decision to build their own shed and water tower.

The London & North Western Railway, having gained access to the town through running powers over the Midland from Wichnor Junction, and the North Stafford from Ashbourne, and seeing their traffic to and from Burton increasing, decided to instal their own engine shed facilities and yard. The L&NWR had built an engine shed at Wichnor Junction in 1854 to provide servicing of engines used to operate the-then leased operations from the South Staffordshire Railway, and during the running powers dispute with the Midland, trains terminated at Wichnor station.

After running powers were obtained and L&NW engines were working into Burton, the company approved the construction of a new shed at Burton to house four engines, in December 1868, but it is not known if this was ever built, nor where it was intended to locate it. However, some fifteen years later, in 1883, the L&NW built its own engine shed alongside Hawkins Lane, with access from the Midland's Hay branch at Hawkins Lane junction.

The Wichnor shed was closed in 1896, as all engine work had been transferred to the new shed in Burton. The shed became known as Burton Horninglow and by the end of the pre-grouping period in 1922, over thirty freight engines were stabled there. The original building had the standard L&NW northlight type of roof (saw-tooth style), but this was replaced with a concrete roof by the LMS in 1946.

The Great Northern Railway installed engine sidings with ash pit, coal and water facilities and a turntable alongside Wetmore Road. There was no engine shed and the facilities were simply for servicing the freight engine turn-round between arrival and departure turns. GNR and later LNER engines working to Burton on passenger services did not use the GN facilities, as to do so would have necessitated complicated and time-consuming light engine workings from and to the passenger station.

8F 48700, one of a batch built at the Southern Railway works at Brighton in 1944. The 1870 roundhouse shows well in this view, and the building on the right was the sand-drying house. Burton Daily Mail

(right) **Former North Staffs 2-4-2T No.1459 was given a 1P power classification by the LMS in the late 1920's in the shed yard. The last of this class was withdrawn in 1934. The second round house building and the Midland signal gantry at Leicester junction are in the background.** H.N.James

Other engine sheds in Burton belonged to the brewery companies, with the largest by far being the Bass & Worthington sheds just behind Guild Street, adjacent to the Midland's Guild St. branch.

The last locomotive shed built, in the early 1960's, was a simple structure to service diesel engines and was located in the steam shed yard alongside Leicester junction. There were proposals for constructing a sizeable diesel depot on this site as the replacement of steam programme gathered pace. However, the breweries were considering alternatives for the movement of beer and empties, and much of the traffic was being moved to road transport. The need for a sizeable diesel depot receded, and the shed as built was more than sufficient to meet the servicing requirements of the small diesel fleet based at Burton. This depot closed in the early 1980's, and was removed from the site in 1996 - as too was the remains of the old steam shed built in 1870.

The types of engines shedded at Burton can be seen from the various illustrations. Throughout the Midland period most were freight engines, with a number of small tank engines specially built by the Midland in the 1870's for the tightly-curved town branch lines. 0-4-4T's were used for the 'Tutbury Jenny' push-pull services, and a handful of 2P 4-4-0 passenger engines were used for Leicester line services, and local passenger turns to Derby and Birmingham. In the post-1922 LMS period, a small number of the larger 2-6-4 tank types were brought in for the Leicester services. The BR period saw three of the standard 2-6-2T 84xxx class allocated to Burton, No's 84006, 84007 and 84008, for the 'Jenny' service, along with 8F 2-8-0's for the heavier freight workings.

The 1870 roundhouse interior on 17th October 1963, after the centre section of the roof had been removed. Another view which says everything about the engine shed - grime all around, oil patches on cobbled walkways, dark and grimy inspection pits, steam and smoke issuing forth from engines being prepared for departure, and a generally cool but nevertheless captivating atmosphere. Author's collection

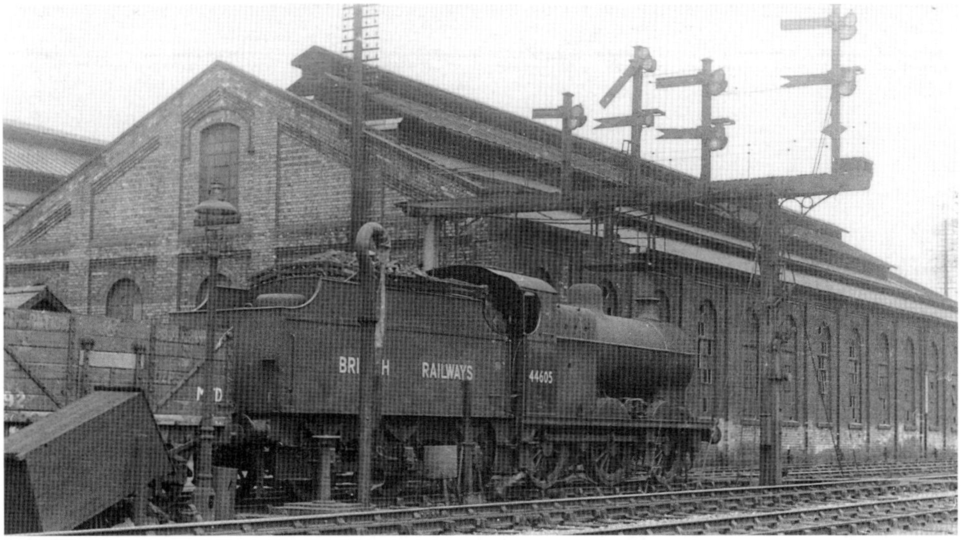

The Midland shed and signal gantry still in use on 2nd June 1950, with LMS built 4F 0-6-0 44605 in early British Railways livery. The Midland gantry and lower quadrant signals were later replaced by a new structure and upper quadrant signals. The late H.C.Casserley

A former L&NW Class D 0-8-0, often referred to as a 'duck-eight', No.9063 carrying a 3A Bescot shedplate, stands in Burton yard on 29th June 1946. These engines worked in from the Lichfield direction. A.Sommerfield collection

A visitor from the LNER, K2 4636, on 19th October 1929, stands on the UP slow line alongside Burton shed, most probably having brought a passenger train in from Derby Friargate, and awaiting turning in readiness for a return working. The proximity of the station and Midland engine shed made for easy turning of LNER engines, rather than the long trek back to Wetmore or Hawkins Lane. W.L.Good

42824, one of the 2-6-0's affectionately known as 'Crabs', stored out of use at Burton on 25th August 1962. This was one of five engines of this class fitted with Lentz cam poppet valve gear in 1931, and altered to Reidinger rotary cam valve gear in January 1954. The cab width of these engines was several inches wider than the width of the tender. Several were shedded at Burton, and in addition to freight turns, they were regular performers on passenger excursion trains. K.C.H.Fairey

(above) **'Jubilee' 4-6-0 engines were regular performers on express services through Burton but it was not until 1957 that the first of this class was allocated to 17B Burton. 45561 SASKATCHEWAN was the first and it spent eighteen months working from the shed. In 1961 eighteen Jubilee's arrived, and many of these were ultimately withdrawn from service and stored out of use. Here 45648 WEMYSS is seen ready for duty on 25th August 1962.** K.C.H.Fairey

(below) **The largest London & North Eastern Railway locomotive was this Beyer Garratt articulated engine, seen in Burton shed yard on 2nd October 1955. It was built in 1925 for rear-end banking of westbound 1,000 ton coal trains up the 2½ mile Worsborough bank between Wath and Penistone. In the 1950's it was based at Bromsgrove to assist northbound trains up the Lickey incline, and on this date it called in at Burton for running repairs. It was numbered 69999 by British Railways and was the largest engine ever to run in Britain. Tractive effort was an incredible 72,940 lb, against the LMS Garratt's 45,620 lb T.E. It is believed this was its first visit to the shed, and here two members of the shed staff (L and R) watch a more venturesome 'Maurice Harper' claiming the bufferbeam for himself.** Patrick Webb

(above and below) **The last engine shed to be built in Burton, seen here in June 1972, with 1000 h.p. diesel electric Bo-Bo D8133 and one of the ubiquitous 0-6-0 shunters. The shed was basically a refuelling facility with inspection pits. Repairs to diesel locomotives were carried out at Derby and Toton.** A.O.Wynn

Ind Coope & Allsopp's had fewer lines through the town, and consequently did not require as many locomotives as Bass & Co., and what they had, was much less frequently photographed. Here, a R&W Hawthorn Leslie & Co. Ltd. of Newcastle-on-Tyne, 0-4-0ST dating from 1876, stands awaiting its next duty in the early 1950's. Author's collection

Truman, Hanbury & Buxton had limited trackwork around it's brewery, situated between Derby Street, and the main railway line - now only a memory, the land now used as a vehicle depot. Their engine was a Peckett 0-4-0, seen here towards the end of rail use by the brewery, prior to closure. R.Newman

These three views show 'Internal user' vehicles with Worthingtons and Bass. The two outside framed vans and three plank wagon are of Midland Railway origin, whilst the three 'Bass Malt' vans are of Great Western Railway origin. Hundreds of wagons owned by the railway companies were shunted around the brewery lines in Burton, and breweries were charged for usage. The breweries purchased old and redundant vans and wagons from the railways, principally the Midland - later the LMS - and used these for internal use, being confined to the privately owned lines and the railway-owned branches through the town. Many cattle wagons were also used on beer trains, and a number of these were also purchased by Bass. As a result of the various purchases, there existed many examples of vans and wagons particularly former MR outside-framed types, right through to the mid-1960's. R.Jeffcoat P.Webb

Ind Coope & Allsopp Ltd., purchased a number of 10-ton bulk tankers from Charles Roberts & Co. Ltd. of Wakefield, and these two views show No.21 as built, and two others in use - both in a white or cream tank livery. Lettering was believed to have been red, with black end-numbers. Author's collection

BURTON'S LOCOMOTIVE BUILDERS

Two locomotive builders were located in the town, one solely involved in manufacture of steam engines, whilst the other built steam, and later petrol and diesel types.

Thornewill & Wareham was building steam engines as early as 1861, and supplying the growing demand from Bass & Co. and other industrial users. Several of their engines lasted through to the end of the brewery railway systems, and they were renowned for their reliability. Early versions were fitted with spectacle plates to give limited protection to the engine crew, and enclosed cabs were fitted later to give much enhanced protection.

The other builder emerged from one of the early motor car manufacturers - Baguley Cars Ltd., which later became Baguley (Engineers) Ltd., and from 1933, E.E.Baguley Ltd. This company developed a world-wide trade, constructing locomotives to suit individual company requirements, and in a range of gauges. It closed towards the end of the 1980's.

(above) **1950s version Baguley diesel engine, a standard 150 hp 26 ton, of the type supplied to Ind Coope & Allsopp Ltd. and Marstons Thompson & Evershed Ltd., at Shobnall, another brewery with a relatively small sidings network.** E.E.Baguley Ltd.

(above) **Bass No.3, a Thornewill & Wareham type originating in 1869, and rebuilt initially in 1909, with a second rebuild including an enclosed cab in 1924. No.3 is seen coming off the Guild Street branch and towards Hay sidings, 18th April 1963.**

(below) **The first diesel locomotive built by Baguley's in Burton is seen here on test, entering the private sidings of Sharp Bros & Knight, Ltd., off the Shobnall branch, believed to be in 1934.** Baguley Drewry

A VARIETY OF TRAFFIC

One of the infamous Deeley 0-6-4 passenger tank engines built in 1907 by the Midland Railway, and later rebuilt with a Belpaire boiler. 2016 is approaching Willington with a through freight from Derby in 1932. The 'W' plate carried on the nearside lamp-iron is belived to have been a 'local trip board', to indicate a destination, most probably Wichnor junction. The wagons are City of Birmingham Gas Works private owner coal wagons, and as there are at least seven, all looking very clean and new, it is probable they were en-route from one of the wagon building companies. Much of the coal for Windsor Street Gas Works in the Saltley area of Birmingham, came from South Derbyshire collieries, and full wagons were despatched to Wichnor, for onward movement to the destination, and empties followed the route in reverse. These engines were nicknamed 'pom poms' by Midland enginemen, and later had the tag of 'Flatiron', both believed to reflect their heavy front end and unstable running

Black 5 4-6-0 44935 brings the empty coaching stock from the Down slow line, into Burton No.1 platform for the 6.35 am excursion to Blackpool on 12th June 1965. The track seen curving off to the right was the route of the first canal branch off the Birmingham & Derby Junction Railway in the early 1840's. Paul A.Forbes

In 1953 a British Railways Standard 2-6-2T type emerged from Crewe works, and three were allocated to Burton for working the 'Tutbury Jenny' service - No's 84006, 84007 and 84008. This view is believed taken in the mid-1950's, with 84006 awaiting departure for the non-stop service direct to Tutbury. Author's collection

Annesley based O1 No.63886 rolls a heavy southbound coal train through Burton on Wednesday 7th June 1961. The train would have originated from the Nottinghamshire coalfield and was probably a load of power station coal. A.Swain.

AND THE FINAL CURTAIN - Views from 10th June 1969......

(top left) **The closed Duke Street crossing signal box, which controlled two quite distinct and adjacent level crossings. The excavator lurkes ominously on the left.** (above) **Looking towards the Dale Street level crossing.** (lower left) **Near Uxbridge Street.** (below) **James Street Junction signal box.** All M.A.King

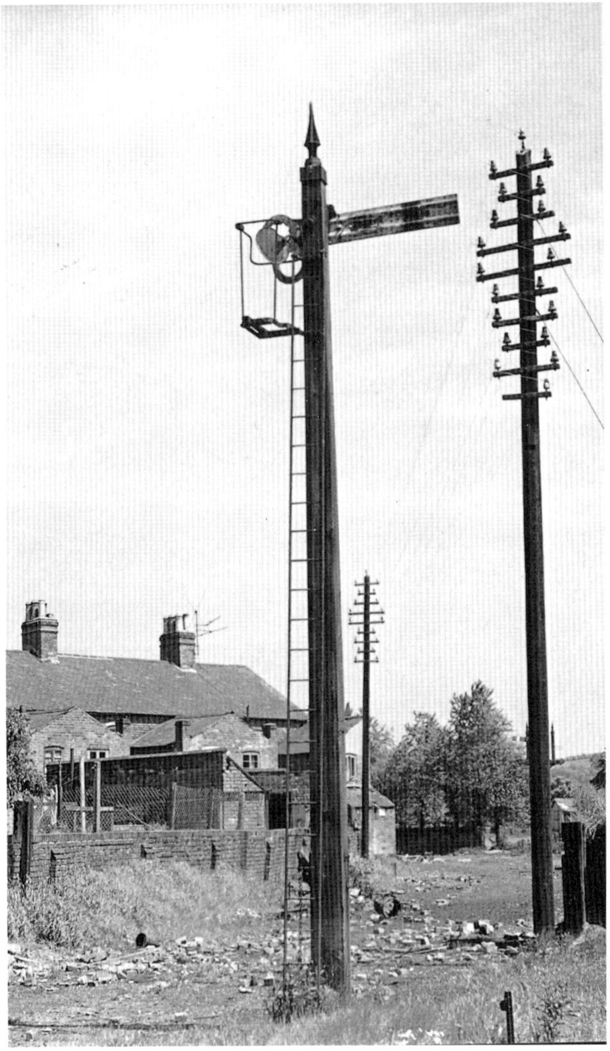

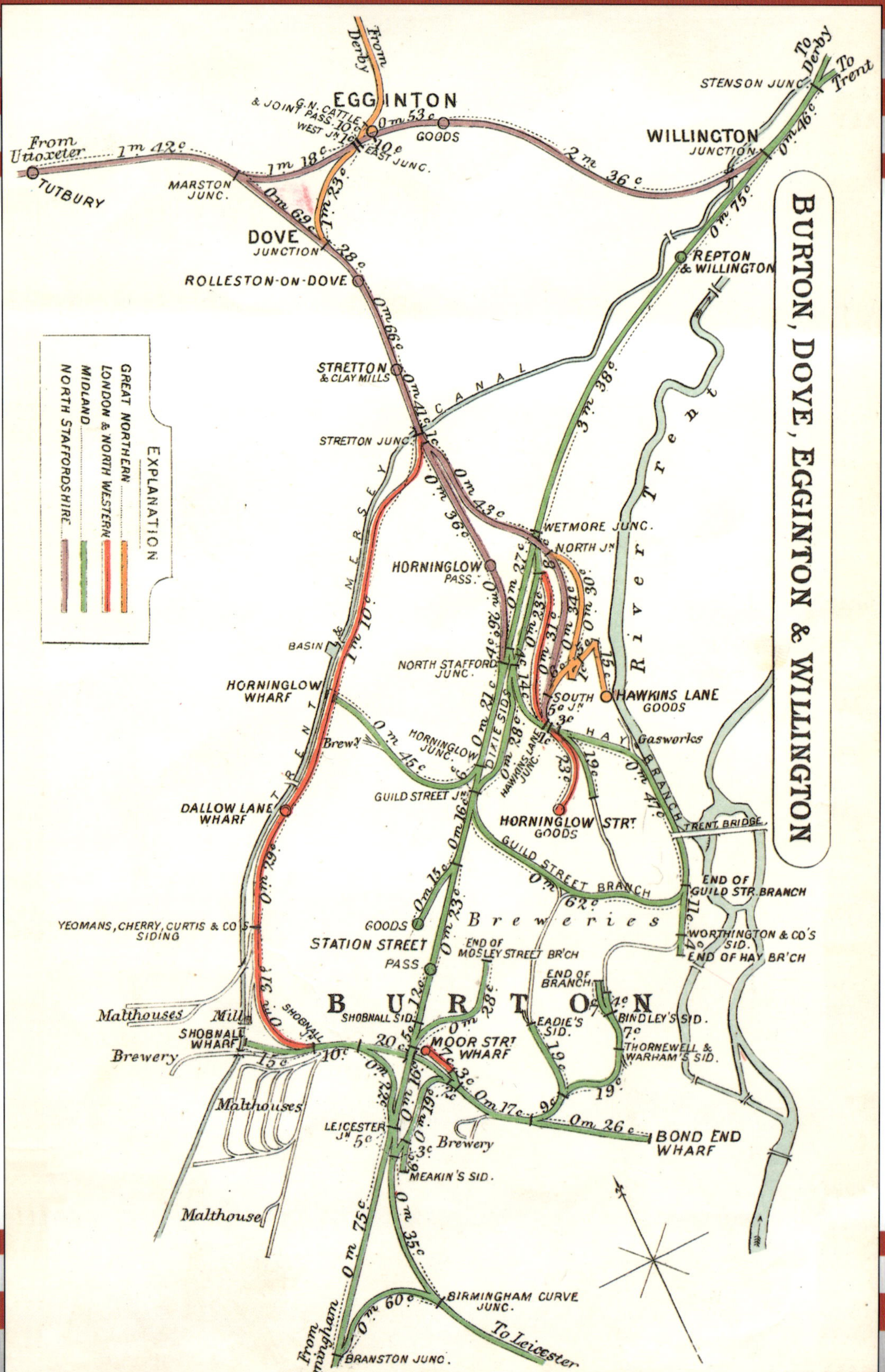

ISBN 1-899-62428-7
9 781899 624287

£12.95

CHALLENGER PUBLICATIONS